THE CIVILIZATION OF CHINA

CHINA

HERBERT A. GILES

For information and contact visit our website at:
IndoEuropeanPublishing.com

The present edition is a revised version of 1921 of this work published by Holt and Company, New York, produced in the current edition with completely new, easy to read format, and is set and proofread by Alfred Aghajanian for Indo-European Publishing.

Cover Design by Indo-European Design Team

ISBN: 978-1-60444-106-2

IndoEuropean
Publishing.com
Los Angeles, CA, USA

PREFACE

The aim of this work is to suggest a rough outline of Chinese civilization from the earliest times down to the present period of rapid and startling transition.

It has been written, primarily, for readers who know little or nothing of China, in the hope that it may succeed in alluring them to a wider and more methodical survey.

H.A.G.

Table of Contents

CHAPTER I

THE FEUDAL AGE

It is a very common thing now-a-days to meet people who are going to "China," which can be reached by the Siberian railway in fourteen or fifteen days. This brings us at once to the question—What is meant by the term China?

Taken in its widest sense, the term includes Mongolia, Manchuria, Eastern Turkestan, Tibet, and the Eighteen Provinces, the whole being equivalent to an area of some five million square miles, that is, considerably more than twice the size of the United States of America. But for a study of manners and customs and modes of thought of the Chinese people, we must confine ourselves to that portion of the whole which is known to the Chinese as the "Eighteen Provinces," and to us as China Proper. This portion of the empire occupies not quite two-fifths of the whole, covering an area of somewhat more than a million and a half square miles. Its chief landmarks may be roughly stated as Peking, the capital, in the north; Canton, the great commercial centre, in the south; Shanghai, on the east; and the Tibetan frontier on the west.

Any one who will take the trouble to look up these four points on a map, representing as they do central points on the four sides of a rough square, will soon realize the absurdity of asking a returning traveler the very much asked question, How do you like China? Fancy asking a Chinaman, who had spent a year or two in England, how he liked Europe! Peking, for instance, stands on the same parallel of latitude as Madrid; whereas Canton coincides similarly with Calcutta. Within the square indicated by the four points enumerated above will be found variations of climate, flowers, fruit, vegetables and animals—not to mention human beings—distributed in very much the same way as in Europe. The climate of Peking is exceedingly dry and bracing; no rain, and hardly any snow, falling between October and April. The really hot weather lasts only for six or eight weeks, about July and August—and even then the nights are always cool; while for six or eight weeks between December and February there may be a couple of feet of ice on the river. Canton, on the other hand, has a tropical climate, with a long damp enervating summer and a short bleak winter. The old story runs that snow has only been seen once in Canton, and then it was thought by the people to be falling cotton-wool.

The northern provinces are remarkable for vast level plains, dotted with villages, the houses of which are built of mud. In the southern provinces will be found long stretches of mountain scenery, vying in loveliness with anything to be seen elsewhere. Monasteries are built high up on the hills, often on almost inaccessible crags; and there the well-to-do Chinaman is wont to escape from the fierce heat of the southern summer. On one particular mountain near Canton, there are said to be no fewer than one hundred of such monasteries, all of which reserve apartments for guests, and are glad to be able to add to their funds by so doing.

In the north of China, Mongolian ponies, splendid mules, and donkeys are seen in large quantities; also the two-humped camel, which carries heavy loads across the plains of Mongolia. In the south, until the advent of the railway, travelers had to choose between the sedan-chair carried on the shoulders of stalwart coolies, or the slower but more comfortable house-boat. Before steamers began to ply on the coast, a candidate for the doctor's degree at the great triennial examination would take three months to travel from Canton to Peking. Urgent dispatches, however, were often forwarded by relays of riders at the rate of two hundred miles a day.

The market in Peking is supplied, among other things, with excellent mutton from a fat-tailed breed of sheep, chiefly for the largely Mohammedan population; but the sheep will not live in southern China, where the goat takes its place. The pig is found everywhere, and represents beef in our market, the latter being extremely unpalatable to the ordinary Chinaman, partly perhaps because Confucius forbade men to slaughter the animal which draws the plough and contributes so much to the welfare of mankind. The staple food, the "bread" of the people in the Chinese Empire, is nominally rice; but this is too costly for the peasant of northern China to import, and he falls back on millet as its substitute. Apples, pears, grapes, melons, and walnuts grow abundantly in the north; the southern fruits are the banana, the orange, the pineapple, the mango, the pomelo, the lichee, and similar fruits of a more tropical character.

Cold storage has been practiced by the Chinese for centuries. Blocks of ice are cut from the river for that purpose; and on a hot summer's day a Peking coolie can obtain an iced drink at an almost infinitesimal cost. Grapes are preserved from autumn until the following May and June by the simple process of sticking the stalk of the bunch into a large hard pear, and putting it away carefully in the ice-house. Even at Ningpo, close to our central point on the eastern coast of China, thin layers of ice are collected from pools and ditches, and successfully stored for use in the following summer.

The inhabitants of the coast provinces are distinguished from the dwellers in the north and in the far interior by a marked alertness of mind and general temperament. The Chinese themselves declare that virtue is associated with mountains, wisdom with water, cynically implying that no

3

one is both virtuous and wise. Between the inhabitants of the various provinces there is little love lost. Northerners fear and hate southerners, and the latter hold the former in infinite scorn and contempt. Thus, when in 1860 the Franco-British force made for Peking, it was easy enough to secure the services of any number of Cantonese, who remained as faithful as though the attack had been directed against some third nationality.

The population of China has never been exactly ascertained. It has been variously estimated by foreign travelers, Sacharoff, in 1842, placing the figure at over four hundred millions. The latest census, taken in 1902, is said to yield a total of four hundred and ten millions. Perhaps three hundred millions would be a juster estimate; even that would absorb no less than one-fifth of the human race. From this total it is easy to calculate that if the Chinese people were to walk past a given point in single file, the procession would never end; long before the last of the three hundred millions had passed by, a new generation would have sprung up to continue the never-ending line. The census, however, is a very old institution with the Chinese; and we learn that in A.D. 156 the total population of the China of those days was returned as a little over fifty millions. In more modern times, the process of taking the census consists in serving out house-tickets to the head of every household, who is responsible for a proper return of all the inmates; but as there is no fixed day for which these tickets are returnable, the results are approximate rather than exact.

Again, it is not uncommon to hear people talking of the Chinese language as if it were a single tongue spoken all over China after a more or less uniform standard. But the fact is that the colloquial is broken up into at least eight dialects, each so strongly marked as to constitute eight languages as different to the ear, one from another, as English, Dutch and German, or French, Spanish, Italian and Portuguese. A Shanghai man, for instance, is unintelligible to a Cantonese, and so on. All officials are obliged, and all of the better educated merchants and others Endeavour, if only for business purposes, to learn something of the dialect spoken at the court of Peking; and this is what is popularly known as "Mandarin." The written language remains the same for the whole empire; which merely means that ideas set down on paper after a uniform system are spoken with different sounds, just as the Arabic numerals are written uniformly in England, France and Germany, but are pronounced in a totally different manner.

The only difficulty of the spoken language, of no matter what dialect, lies in the "tones," which simply means the different intonations which may be given to one and the same sound, thus producing so many entirely different meanings. But for these tones, the colloquial of China would be absurdly easy, inasmuch as there is no such thing as grammar, in the sense of gender, number, case, mood, tense, or any of the variations we understand by that term. Many amusing examples are current of blunders committed by faulty speakers, such as that of the student who told his servant to bring him a goose, when what he really wanted was some salt, both goose and salt having the same sound, *yen*, but quite different intonations. The following specimen has the advantage of being true. A British official reported to the Foreign Office that the people of Tientsin were in the habit of shouting after foreigners, "Mao-tsu, mao-tsu" (pronounced *mowdza*, *ow* as in *how*), from which he gathered that they were much struck by the head-gear of the barbarian. Now, it is a fact that *mao-tsu*, uttered with a certain intonation, means a hat; but with another intonation, it means "hairy one," and the latter, referring to the big beards of foreigners, was the meaning intended to be conveyed. This epithet is still to be heard, and is often preceded by the adjective "red."

The written characters, known to have been in use for the past three thousand years, were originally rude pictures, as of men, birds, horses, dogs, houses, the numerals (one, two, three, four), etc., etc., and it is still possible to trace in the modified modern forms of these characters more or less striking resemblances to the objects intended. The next step was to put two or more characters together, to express by their combination an abstract idea, as, for instance, a *hand* holding a *rod* = father; but of course this simple process did not carry the Chinese very far, and they soon managed to hit on a joint picture and phonetic system, which enabled them to multiply characters indefinitely, new compounds being formed for use as required. It is thus that new characters can still be produced, if necessary, to express novel objects or ideas. The usual plan, however, is to combine existing terms in such a way as to suggest what is wanted. For instance, in preference to inventing a separate character for the piece of ordnance known as a "mortar," the Chinese, with an eye to its peculiar pose, gave it the appropriate name of a "frog gun."

Again, just as the natives and the dialects of the various parts of China differ one from another, although fundamentally the same people and the same language, so do the manners and customs differ to such an extent that habits of life and ceremonial regulations which prevail in one part of the empire do not necessarily prevail in another. Yet once more it will be found that the differences which appear irreconcilable at first, do not affect what is essential, but apply rather to matters of detail. Many travelers and others have described as customs of the Chinese customs which, as presented, refer to a part of China only, and not to the whole. For instance, the ornamental ceremonies connected with marriage vary in different provinces; but there is a certain ceremony, equivalent in one sense to signing the register, which is almost essential to every marriage contract. Bride and bridegroom must kneel down and call God to witness; they also pledge each other in wine from two cups joined together by a red string. Red is the color for joy, as white is the color for mourning. Chinese note-paper is always ruled with red lines or stamped with a red picture. One

Chinese official who gave a dinner-party in foreign style, even went so far as to paste a piece of red paper on to each dinner-napkin, in order to counteract the unpropitious influence of white.

Reference has been made above to journeys performed by boat. In addition to the Yangtsze and the Yellow River or Hoang ho (pronounced *Hwong haw*), two of the most important rivers in the world, China is covered with a network of minor streams, which in southern China form the chief lines of transport. The Yangtsze is nothing more than a huge navigable river, crossing China Proper from west to east. The Yellow River, which, with the exception of a great loop to the north, runs on nearly parallel lines of latitude, has long been known as "China's Sorrow," and has been responsible for enormous loss of life and property. Its current is so swift that ordinary navigation is impossible, and to cross it in boats is an undertaking of considerable difficulty and danger. It is so called from the yellowness of its water, caused by the vast quantity of mud which is swept down by its rapid current to the sea; hence, the common saying, "When the Yellow River runs clear," as an equivalent of the Greek Kalends. The huge embankments, built to confine it to a given course, are continually being forced by any unusual press of extra water, with enormous damage to property and great loss of life, and from time to time this river has been known to change its route altogether, suddenly diverging, almost at a right angle. Up to the year 1851 the mouth of the river was to the south of the Shantung promontory, about lat. 34 N.; then, with hardly any warning, it began to flow to the north-east, finding an outlet to the north of the Shantung promontory, about lat. 38 N.

A certain number of connecting links have been formed between the chief lines of water communication, in the shape of artificial cuttings; but there is nothing worthy the name of canal except the rightly named Grand Canal, called by the Chinese the "river of locks," or alternatively the "transport river," because once used to convey rice from the south to Peking. This gigantic work, designed and executed in the thirteenth century by the Emperor Kublai Khan, extended to about six hundred and fifty miles in length, and completed an almost unbroken water communication between Peking and Canton. As a wonderful engineering feat it is indeed more than matched by the famous Great Wall, which dates back to a couple of hundred years before Christ, and which has been glorified as the last trace of man's handiwork on the globe to fade from the view of an imaginary person receding into space. Recent exploration shows that this wall is about eighteen hundred miles in length, stretching from a point on the seashore somewhat east of Peking, to the northern frontier of Tibet. Roughly speaking, it is twenty-two feet in height by twenty feet in breadth; at intervals of a hundred yards are towers forty feet high, the whole being built originally of brick, of which in some parts but mere traces now remain. Nor is this the only great wall; ruins of other walls on a considerable scale have lately been brought to light, the object of all being one and the same—to keep back the marauding Tartars.

Over the length and breadth of their boundless empire, with all its varying climates and inhabitants, the Chinese people are free to travel, for business or pleasure, at their own sweet will, and to take up their abode at any spot without let or hindrance. No passports are required; neither is any ordinary citizen obliged to possess other papers of identification. Chinese inns are not exposed to the annoyance of domiciliary visits with reference to their clients for the time being; and so long as the latter pay their way, and refrain from molesting others, they will usually be free from molestation themselves. The Chinese, however, are not fond of travelling; they love their homes too well, and they further dread the inconveniences and dangers attached to travel in many other parts of the world. Boatmen, carters, and innkeepers have all of them bad reputations for extortionate charges; and the traveler may sometimes happen upon a "black inn," which is another name for a den of thieves. Still there have been many who travelled for the sake of beautiful scenery, or in order to visit famous spots of historical interest; not to mention the large body of officials who are constantly on the move, passing from post to post.

Among those who believe that every nation must have reached its present quarters from some other distant parts of the world, must be reckoned a few students of the ancient history of China. Coincidences in language and in manners and customs, mostly of a shadowy character, have led some to suggest Babylonia as the region from which the Chinese migrated to the land where they are now found. The Chinese possess authentic records of an indisputably early past, but throughout these records there is absolutely no mention, not even a hint, of any migration of the kind.

Tradition places the Golden Age of China so far back as three thousand years before Christ; for a sober survey of China's early civilization, it is not necessary to push further back than the tenth century B.C. We shall find evidence of such an advanced state of civilization at that later date as to leave no doubt of a very remote antiquity.

The China of those days, known even then as the Middle Kingdom, was a mere patch on the empire of to-day. It lay, almost lozenge-shaped, between the 34th and 40th parallels of latitude north, with the upper point of the lozenge resting on the modern Peking, and the lower on Si-an Fu in Shensi, whither the late Empress Dowager fled for safety during the Boxer rising in 1900. The ancient autocratic Imperial system had recently been disestablished, and a feudal system had taken its place. The country was divided up into a number of vassal states of varying size and importance, ruled each by its own baron, who swore allegiance to the sovereign of the Royal State. The relations, however, which came to subsist, as time went on, between these states, sovereign and vassal alike, as described in contemporary annals, often remind the reader of the relations which prevailed between the various political divisions of ancient Greece. The rivalries of Athens and Sparta, whose capitals were only one hundred and fifty miles apart—though a perusal of Thucydides makes one feel that at least half the world was involved—find their exact equivalent in the jealousies and animosities which stirred the feudal states of ancient China, and in the disastrous campaigns and bloody battles which the states fought with one another. We read of chariots and horsemanship; of feats of arms and deeds of individual heroism; of forced marches, and of night attacks in which the Chinese soldier was gagged with a kind of wooden bit, to prevent talking in the ranks; of territory annexed and re-conquered, and of the violent deaths of rival rulers by poison or the dagger of the assassin.

When the armies of these states went into battle they formed a line, with the bowmen on the left and the spearmen on the right flank. The centre was occupied by chariots, each drawn by either three or four horses harnessed abreast. Swords, daggers, shields, iron-headed clubs some five to six feet in length and weighing from twelve to fifteen pounds, huge iron hooks, drums, cymbals, gongs, horns, banners and streamers innumerable, were also among the equipment of war. Beacon-fires of wolves' dung were lighted to announce the approach of an enemy and summon the inhabitants to arms. Quarter was rarely if ever given, and it was customary to cut the ears from the bodies of the slain. Parleys were conducted and terms of peace arranged under the shelter of a banner of truce, upon which two words were inscribed—"Stop fighting."

The beacon-fires above mentioned, very useful for summoning the feudal barons to the rescue in case of need, cost one sovereign his throne. He had a beautiful concubine, for the sake of whose company he neglected the affairs of government. The lady was of a melancholy turn, never being seen to smile. She said she loved the sound of rent silk, and to gratify her whim many fine pieces of silk were torn to shreds. The king offered a thousand ounces of gold to any one who would make her laugh; whereupon his chief minister suggested that the beacon-fires should be lighted to summon the feudal nobles with their armies, as though the royal house were in danger. The trick succeeded; for in the hurry-scurry that ensued the impassive girl positively laughed outright. Later on, when a real attack was made upon the capital by barbarian hordes, and the beacon-fires were again lighted, this time in stern reality, there was no response from the insulted nobles. The king was killed, and his concubine strangled herself.

Meanwhile, a high state of civilization was enjoyed by these feudal peoples, when not engaged in cutting each other's throats. They lived in thatched houses constructed of rammed earth and plaster, with beaten floors on which dry grass was strewn as carpet. Originally accustomed to sit on mats, they introduced chairs and tables at an early date; they drank an ardent spirit with their carefully cooked food, and wore robes of silk. Ballads were sung, and dances were performed, on ceremonial and festive occasions; hunting and fishing and agriculture were occupations for the men, while the women employed themselves in spinning and weaving. There were casters of bronze vessels, and workers in gold, silver, and iron; jade and other stones were cut and polished for ornaments. The written language was already highly developed, being much the same as we now find it. Indeed, the chief difference lies in the form of the characters, just as an old English text differs in form from a text of the present day. What we may call the syntax of the language has remained very much the same; and phrases from the old ballads of three thousand years ago, which have passed into the colloquial, are still readily understood, though of course pronounced according to the requirements of modern speech. We can no more say how Confucius (551-479 B.C.) pronounced Chinese, than we can say how Miltiades pronounced Greek when addressing his soldiers before the battle of Marathon (490 B.C.). The "books" which were read in ancient China consisted of thin slips of wood or bamboo, on which the characters were written by means of a pencil of wood or bamboo, slightly frayed at the end, so as to pick up a colored liquid and transfer it to the tablets as required. Until recently, it was thought that the Chinese scratched their words on tablets of bamboo with a knife, but now we know that the knife was only used for scratching out, when a character was wrongly written.

The art of healing was practiced among the Chinese in their pre-historic times, but the earliest efforts of a methodical character, of which we have any written record, belong to the period with which we are now dealing. There is indeed a work, entitled "Plain Questions," which is attributed to a legendary emperor of the Golden Age, who interrogates one of his ministers on the cause and cure of all kinds of diseases; as might be expected, it is not of any real value, nor can its date be carried back beyond a few centuries B.C.

Physicians of the feudal age classified diseases under the four seasons of the year: headaches and neuralgic affections under *spring*, skin diseases of all kinds under *summer*, fevers and agues under *autumn*, and bronchial and pulmonary complaints under *winter*. They treated the various complaints that fell under these headings by suitable doses of one or more ingredients taken from the five classes of drugs, derived from herbs, trees, living creatures, minerals, and grains, each of which class contained medicines of five flavors, with special properties: *sour* for nourishing the bones, *acid* for nourishing the muscles, *salt* for nourishing the blood-vessels, *bitter* for nourishing general vitality, and *sweet* for nourishing the flesh. The pulse has always been very much to the front in the treatment of disease; there are at least twenty-four varieties of pulse with which every doctor is supposed to be familiar, and some eminent doctors have claimed to distinguish no fewer than seventy-two. In the "Plain Questions" there is a sentence which points towards the circulation of the blood,—"All the blood is under the jurisdiction of the heart," a point beyond which the Chinese never seem to have pushed their investigations; but of this curious feature in their civilization, later on.

It was under the feudal system, perhaps a thousand years before Christ, that the people of China began to possess family names. Previous to that time there appear to have been tribal or clan names; these however were not in ordinary use among the individual members of each clan, who were known by their personal names only, bestowed upon them in childhood by their parents. Gradually, it became customary to prefix to the personal name a surname, adopted generally from the name of the place where the family lived, sometimes from an appellation or official title of a distinguished ancestor; places in China never take their names from individuals, as with us, and consequently there are no such names as Faringdon or Gislingham, the homes of the Fearings or Gislings of old. Thus, to use English terms, a boy who had been called "Welcome" by his parents might prefix the name of the place, Cambridge, where he was born, and call himself Cambridge Welcome, the surname always coming first in Chinese, as, for instance, in Li Hung-Chang. The Manchus, it must be remembered, have no surnames; that is to say, they do not use their clan or family names, but call themselves by their personal names only.

Chinese surnames, other than place names, are derived from a variety of sources: from nature, as River, Stone, Cave; from animals, as Bear, Sheep, Dragon; from birds, as Swallow, Pheasant; from the body, as Long-ears, Squint-eye; from colors, as Black, White; from trees and flowers, as Hawthorn, Leaf, Reed, Forest; and others, such as Rich, East, Sharp, Hope, Duke, Stern, Tepid, Money, etc. By the fifth century before Christ, the use of surnames had definitely become established for all classes, whereas in Europe surnames were not known until about the twelfth century after Christ, and even then were confined to persons of wealth and position. There is a small Chinese book, studied by every schoolboy and

13

entitled *The Hundred Surnames*, the word "hundred" being commonly used in a generally comprehensive sense. It actually contains about four hundred of the names which occur most frequently.

About two hundred and twenty years before Christ, the feudal system came to an end. One aggressive state gradually swallowed up all the others; and under the rule of its sovereign, China became once more an empire, and such it has ever since remained. But although always an empire, the throne, during the past two thousand years, has passed many times from one house to another.

The extraordinary man who led his state to victory over each rival in turn, and ultimately mounted the throne to rule over a united China, finds his best historical counterpart in Napoleon. He called himself the First Emperor, and began by sending an army of 300,000 men to fight against an old and dreaded enemy to the north, recently identified beyond question with the Huns. He dispatched a fleet to search for some mysterious islands off the coast, thought by some to be the islands which form Japan. He built the Great Wall, to a great extent by means of convict labor, malefactors being condemned to long terms of penal servitude on the works. His copper coinage was so uniformly good that the cowry disappeared altogether from commerce during his reign. Above all things he desired to impart a fresh stimulus to literary effort, but he adopted singularly unfortunate means to secure this desirable end; for, listening to the insidious flattery of courtiers, he determined that literature should begin anew with his reign. He therefore determined to destroy all existing books, finally deciding to spare those connected with three important departments of human knowledge: namely, (1) works which taught the people to plough, sow, reap, and provide food for the race; (2) works on the use of drugs and on the healing art; and (3) works on the various methods of foretelling the future which might lead men to act in accordance with, and not in opposition to, the eternal fitness of things as seen in the operations of Nature. Stringent orders were issued accordingly, and many scholars were put to death for concealing books in the hope that the storm would blow over. Numbers of valuable works perished in a vast conflagration of books, and the only wonder is that any were preserved, with the exception of the three classes specified above.

In 210 B.C. the First Emperor died, and his youngest son was placed upon the throne with the title of Second Emperor. The latter began by carrying out the funeral arrangements of his father, as described about a century later by the first and greatest of China's historians:—

"On the 9th moon the First Emperor was buried in Mount Li, which in the early days of his reign he had caused to be tunneled and prepared with that view. Then, when he had consolidated the empire, he employed his soldiery, to the number of 700,000, to bore down to the Three Springs (that is, until water was reached), and there a firm foundation was laid and the sarcophagus placed thereon. Rare objects and costly jewels were collected from the palaces and from the various officials, and were carried thither and stored in huge quantities. Artificers were ordered to construct mechanical crossbows, which, if any one were to enter, would immediately discharge their arrows. With the aid of quicksilver, rivers were made—the Yangtsze, the Yellow River, and the great ocean—the metal being made to flow from one into the other by machinery. On the roof were delineated the constellations of the sky, on the floor the geographical divisions of the earth. Candles were made from the fat of the man-fish (walrus), calculated to last for a very long time. The Second Emperor said: 'It is not fitting that the concubines of my late father who are without children should leave him now;' and accordingly he ordered them to accompany the dead monarch into the next world, those who thus perished being many in number. When the internment was completed, some one suggested that the workmen who had made the machinery and concealed the treasure knew the great value of the latter, and that the secret would leak out. Therefore, so soon as the ceremony was over, and the path giving access to the sarcophagus had been blocked up at its innermost end, the outside gate at the entrance to this path was let fall, and the mausoleum was effectually closed, so that not one of the workmen escaped. Trees and grass were then planted around, that the spot might look like the rest of the mountain."

The career of the Second Emperor finds an apt parallel in that of Richard Cromwell, except that the former was put to death, after a short and inglorious reign. Then followed a dynasty which has left an indelible mark upon the civilization as well as on the recorded history of China. A peasant, by mere force of character, succeeded after a three-years' struggle in establishing himself upon the throne, 206 B.C., and his posterity, known as the House of Han, ruled over China for four hundred years, accidentally divided into two nearly equal portions by the Christian era, about which date there occurred a temporary usurpation of the throne which for some time threatened the stability of the dynasty in the direct line of succession. To this date, the more northern Chinese have no prouder title than that of a "son of Han."

During the whole period of four hundred years the empire cannot be said to have enjoyed complete tranquility either at home or abroad. There were constant wars with the Tartar tribes on the north, against whom the Great Wall proved to be a somewhat ineffectual barrier. Also with the Huns, the forbears of the Turks, who once succeeded in shutting up the founder of the dynasty in one of his own cities, from which he only escaped by a stratagem to be related in another connection. There were in addition wars with Korea, the ultimate conquest of which led to the discovery of Japan, then at a low level of civilization and unable to enter into official relations with China until A.D. 57, when an embassy was sent for the first time. Those who are accustomed to think of the Chinese as an eminently unwarlike nation will perhaps be surprised to

16

hear that before the end of the second century B.C. they had carried their victorious arms far away into Central Asia, annexing even the Pamirs and Kokand to the empire. The wild tribes of modern Yunnan were reduced to subjection, and their territory may further be considered as added from about this period.

At home, the eunuchs gave an immense deal of trouble by their restless spirit of intrigue; besides which, for nearly twenty years the Imperial power was in the hands of a famous usurper, named Wang Mang (pronounced *Wahng Mahng*), who had secured it by the usual means of treachery and poison, to lose it on the battle-field and himself to perish shortly afterwards in a revolt of his own soldiery. But the most remarkable of all events connected with the Han dynasty was the extended revival of learning and authorship. Texts of the Confucian Canon were rescued from hiding-places in which they had been concealed at the risk of death; editing committees were appointed, and immense efforts were made to repair the mischief sustained by literature at the hands of the First Emperor. The scholars of the day expounded the teachings of Confucius as set forth in these texts; and although their explanations were set aside in the twelfth century, when an entirely new set of interpretations became (and remain) the accepted standard for all students, it is mostly due to those early efforts that the Confucian Canon has exercised such a deep and lasting influence over the minds of the Chinese people. Unfortunately, it soon became the fashion to discover old texts, and many works are now in circulation which have no claim whatever to the antiquity to which they pretend.

During the four hundred years of Han supremacy the march of civilization went steadily forward. Paper and ink were invented, and also the camel's-hair brush, both of which gave a great impetus to the arts of writing and painting, the latter being still in a very elementary stage. The custom of burying slaves with the dead was abolished early in the dynasty. The twenty-seven months of

17

mourning for parents—nominally three years, as is now again the rule—was reduced to a more manageable period of twenty-seven days. Literary degrees were first established, and perpetual hereditary rank was conferred upon the senior descendant of Confucius in the male line, which has continued in unbroken succession down to the present day. The head of the Confucian clan is now a duke, and resides in a palace, taking rank with, if not before, the highest provincial authorities.

The extended military campaigns in Central Asia during this period brought China into touch with Bactria, then an outlying province of ancient Greece. From this last source, the Chinese learnt many things which are now often regarded as of purely native growth. They imported the grape, and made from it a wine which was in use for many centuries, disappearing only about two or three hundred years ago. Formerly dependent on the sun-dial alone, the Chinese now found themselves in possession of the water-clock, specimens of which are still to be seen in full working order, whereby the division of the day into twelve two-hour periods was accurately determined. The calendar was regulated anew, and the science of music was reconstructed; in fact, modern Chinese music may be said to approximate closely to the music of ancient Greece. Because of the difference of scale, Chinese music does not make any appeal to Western ears; at any rate, not in the sense in which it appealed to Confucius, who has left it on record that after listening to a certain melody he was so affected as not to be able to taste meat for three months.

CHAPTER II

LAW AND GOVERNMENT

In the earliest ages of which history professes to take cognizance, persons who wished to dispose of their goods were obliged to have recourse to barter. By and by shells were adopted as a medium of exchange, and then pieces of stamped silk, linen, and deerskin. These were followed by circular discs of copper, pierced with a round hole, the forerunners of the ordinary copper coins of a century or two later, which had square holes, and bore inscriptions, as they still do in the present day. Money was also cast in the shape of "knives" and of "trouser," by which names specimens of this early coinage (mostly fakes) are known to connoisseurs. Some of these were beautifully finished, and even inlaid with gold. Early in the ninth century, bills of exchange came into use; and from the middle of the twelve century paper money became quite common, and is still in general use all over China, notes being issued in some places for amounts less even than a shilling.

Measures of length and capacity were fixed by the Chinese after an exceedingly simple process. The grain of millet, which is fairly uniform in size, was taken as the unit of both. Ten of these grains, laid end-ways, formed the inch, ten of which made a foot, and ten feet a *chang*. The decimal system has always prevailed in China, with one curious exception: sixteen ounces make a pound. How this came to be so does not appear to be known; but in this case it is the pound which is the unit of weight, and not the lower denomination. The word which for more than twenty centuries signified "pound" to the Chinese, was originally the rude picture of an axe-head; and there is no doubt that axe-heads, being all of the same size, were used in weighing commodities, and were subsequently split, for convenience's sake, into sixteen equal parts, each about one-third heavier than the English ounce. For measures of capacity, we must revert to the millet-grain, a fixed number of which set the standard for Chinese pints and quarts. The result of this rule-of-thumb calculation has been that weights and measures vary all over the empire, although there actually exist an official foot, pound and pint, as recognized by the Chinese government. In one and the same city a tailor's foot will differ from a carpenter's foot, an oilman's pint from a spirit-merchant's pint, and so on. The final appeal is to local custom.

With the definitive establishment of the monarchy, two hundred years before the Christian era, a system of government was inaugurated which has proceeded, so far as essentials are concerned, upon almost uniform lines down to the present day.

It is an ancient and well-recognized principle in China, that every inch of soil belongs to the sovereign; consequently, all land is held on consideration of a land-tax payable to the emperor, and so long as this tax is forthcoming, the land in question is practically freehold, and can be passed by sale from hand to hand for a small conveyancing fee to the local authorities who stamp the deeds. Thus, the foreign concessions or settlements in China were not sold or parted with in any way by the Chinese; they were "leased in perpetuity" so long as the ground-rent is paid, and remain for all municipal and such purposes under the uncontrolled administration of the nation which leased them. The land-tax may be regarded as the backbone of Chinese finance; but although nominally collected at a fixed rate, it is subject to fluctuations due to bad harvests and like visitations, in which cases the tax is accepted at a lower rate, in fact at any rate the people can afford to pay.

The salt and other monopolies, together with the customs, also contribute an important part of China's revenue. There is the old native customs service, with its stations and barriers all over the empire, and the foreign customs service, as established at the treaty ports only, in order to deal with shipments on foreign vessels trading with China. The traditional and well-marked lines of taxation are freely accepted by the people; any attempt, however, to increase the amounts to be levied, or to introduce new charges of any kind, unless duly authorized by the people themselves, would be at once sternly resisted. As a matter of fact, the authorities never run any such risks. It is customary, when absolutely necessary, and possibly desirable, to increase old or to introduce new levies, for the local authorities to invite the leading merchants and others concerned to a private conference; and only when there is a general consent of all parties do the officials venture to put forth proclamations saying that such and such a tax will be increased or imposed, as the case may be. Any other method may lead to disastrous results. The people refuse to pay; and coercion is met at once by a general closing of shops and stoppage of trade, or, in more serious cases, by an attack on the official residence of the offending mandarin, who soon sees his house looted and leveled with the ground. In other words, the Chinese people tax themselves.

The nominal form of government, speaking without reference to the new constitution which will be dealt with later on, is an irresponsible autocracy; its institutions are likewise autocratic in form, but democratic in operation. The philosopher, Mencius (372-289 B.C.), placed the people first, the gods second, and the sovereign third, in the scale of national importance; and this classification has sunk deep into the minds of the Chinese during more than two thousand years past. What the people in China will not stand is injustice; at the same time they will live contentedly under harsh laws which they have at one time or another imposed upon themselves.

Each of the great dynasties has always begun with a Penal Code of its own, based upon that of the outgoing dynasty, but tending to be more and more humane in character as time goes on. The punishments in old days were atrocious in their severity; the Penal Code of the present dynasty, which came into force some two hundred and fifty years ago, has been pronounced by competent judges to take a very high rank indeed. It was introduced to replace a much harsher code which had been in operation under the Ming dynasty, and contains the nominally immutable laws of the empire, with such modifications and restrictions as have been authorized from time to time by Imperial edict. Still farther back in Chinese history, we come upon punishments of ruthless cruelty, such as might be expected to prevail in times of lesser culture and refinement. Two thousand years ago, the Five Punishments were—branding on the forehead, cutting off the nose, cutting off the feet, mutilation, and death; for the past two hundred and fifty years, these have been— beating with the light bamboo, beating with the heavy bamboo, transportation for a certain period, banishment to a certain distance, and death, the last being subdivided into strangling and decapitation, according to the gravity of the offence.

Two actual instruments of torture are mentioned, one for compressing the ankle-bones, and the other for squeezing the fingers, to be used if necessary to extort a confession in charges of robbery and homicide, confession being regarded as essential to the completion of the record. The application, however, of these tortures is fenced round in such a way as to impose great responsibility upon the presiding magistrate; and in addition to the risk of official impeachment, there is the more dreaded certainty of loss of influence and of popular esteem. Mention is made in the code of the so-called "lingering death," according to which first one arm is chopped off, then the other; the two legs follow in the same way; two slits are made on the breast, and the heart is torn out; decapitation finishes the proceedings. It is worthy of note that, although many foreigners have been present from time to time at public executions, occasionally when the "lingering death" has been announced, not one has established it as a fact beyond a doubt that such a process has ever been carried out. Not only that; it is also well known that condemned criminals are allowed to purchase of themselves, or through their friends, if they have any, spirits or opium with which to fortify their courage at the last moment. There is indeed a tradition that stupefying drinks are served out by the officials to the batches of malefactors as they pass to the execution ground at Peking. It would still remain to find executioners capable of performing in cold blood such a disgusting operation as the "lingering death" is supposed to be. The ordinary Chinaman is not a fiend; he does not gloat in his peaceful moments, when not under the influence of extreme excitement, over bloodshed and cruelty.

The generally lenient spirit in which the Penal Code of China was conceived is either widely unknown, or very often ignored. For instance, during the excessive summer heats certain punishments are mitigated, and others remitted altogether. Prompt surrender and acknowledgment of an offence, before it is otherwise discovered, entitles the offender, with some exceptions, to a full and free pardon; as also does restitution of stolen property to its owner by a repentant thief; while a criminal guilty of two or more offences can be punished only to the extent of the principal charge. Neither are the near relatives, nor even the servants, of a guilty man, punishable for concealing his crime and assisting him to escape. Immense allowances are made for the weakness of human nature, in all of which may be detected the tempering doctrines of the great Sage. A feudal baron was boasting to Confucius that in his part of the country the people were so upright that a son would give evidence against a father who had stolen a sheep. "With us," replied

Confucius, "the father screens the son, and the son screens the father; that is real uprightness." To another questioner, a man in high authority, who complained of the number of thieves, the Master explained that this was due to the greed of the upper classes. "But for this greed," he added, "even if you paid people to steal, they would not do so." To the same man, who inquired his views on capital punishment, Confucius replied: "What need is there for capital punishment at all? If your aims are worthy, the people also will be worthy."

There are many other striking features of the Penal Code. No marriage, for instance, may be contracted during the period of mourning for parents, which in theory extends to three full years, but in practice is reckoned at twenty-seven months; neither may musical instruments be played by near relatives of the dead. During the same period, no mandarin may hold office, but must retire into private life; though the observance of this rule is often dispensed with in the case of high officials whose presence at their posts may be of considerable importance. In such cases, by special grace of the emperor, the period of retirement is cut down to three months, or even to one.

The death of an emperor is followed by a long spell of national tribulation. For one hundred days no man may have his head shaved, and no woman may wear head ornaments. For twelve months there may be no marrying or giving in marriage among the official classes, a term which is reduced to one hundred days for the public at large. The theatres are supposed to remain closed for a year, but in practice they shut only for one hundred days. Even thus great hardships are entailed upon many classes of the community, especially upon actors and barbers, who might be in danger of actual starvation but for the common-sense of their rulers coupled with the common rice-pot at home.

The law forbidding marriage between persons of the same surname is widely, but not universally, in operation. No

Smith may marry a Smith; no Jones may marry a Jones; the reason of course being that all of the same surname are regarded as members of the same family. However, there are large districts in certain parts of China where the people are one and all of the surname, and where it would be a great hardship—not to mention the impossibility of enforcing the law—if intermarriages of the kind were prohibited. Consequently, they are allowed, but only if the contracting parties are so distantly related that, according to the legal table of affinity, they would not wear mourning for one another in case of death—in other words, not related at all. The line of descent is now traced through the males, but there is reason to believe that in early days, as is found to be often the case among uncivilized tribes, the important, because more easily recognizable, parent was the mother. Thus it is illegal for first cousins of the same surname to marry, and legal if the surnames are different; in the latter case, however, centuries of experience have taught the Chinese to frown upon such unions as undesirable in the extreme.

The Penal Code forbids water burial, and also cremation; but it is permitted to the children of a man dying at a great distance to consume their father's corpse with fire if positively unable to bring it back for ordinary burial in his native district. The idea is that with the aid of fire immediate communication is set up with the spirit-world, and that the spirit of the deceased is thus enabled to reach his native place, which would be impossible were the corpse to remain intact. Hence the horror of dying abroad, common to all Chinese, and only faced if there is a reasonable probability that their remains will be carried back to the ancestral home.

In spite of the above law, the cremation of Buddhist priests is universal, and the practice is tolerated without protest. Priests who are getting on in years, or who are stricken with a mortal disease, are compelled by rule to move into a certain part of their monastery, known as the Abode of a Long Old Age, in which they are required—not to die, for death does not come to a good priest, but—to enter into Nirvana, which is a sublime state of conscious freedom from all mental and physical disturbance, not to be adequately described in words. At death, the priest is placed in a chair, his chin supported by a crutch, and then put into a wooden box, which on the appointed day is carried in procession, with streaming banners, through the monastery, and out into the cremation-ground attached, his brother priests chanting all the while that portion of the Buddhist liturgies set apart as the service for the dead, but which being in Pali, not a single one of them can understand. There have, of course, been many highly educated priests at one time and another during the long reign of Buddhism in China; but it is safe to say that they are no longer to be met with in the present day. The Buddhist liturgies have been written out in Chinese characters which reproduce the sounds of the original Indian language, and these the priests learn by heart without understanding a word of their meaning. The box with the dead man in it is now hoisted to the top of a funeral pyre, which has been well drenched with oil, and set alight; and when the fire has burnt out, the ashes are reverently collected and placed in an urn, which is finally deposited in a mausoleum kept for that purpose.

Life is remarkably safe in China. No man can be executed until his name has been submitted to the emperor, which of course means to his ministers at the capital. The Chinese, however, being, as has been so often stated, an eminently practical people, understand that certain cases admit of no delay; and to prevent the inevitable lynching of such criminals as kidnappers, rebels, and others, caught red-handed, high officials are entrusted with the power of life and death, which they can put into immediate operation, always taking upon themselves full responsibility for their acts. The essential is to allay any excitement of the populace, and to preserve the public peace.

26

In the general administration of the law great latitude is allowed, and injustice is rarely inflicted by a too literal interpretation of the Code. Stealing is of course a crime, yet no Chinese magistrate would dream of punishing a hungry man for simple theft of food, even if such a case were ever brought into court. Cake-sellers keep a sharp eye on their wares; farmers and market-gardeners form associates for mutual protection, and woe to the thief who gets caught—his punishment is short and sharp. Litigation is not encouraged, even by such facilities as ought to be given to persons suffering wrongs; there is no bar, or legal profession, and persons who assist plaintiffs or defendants in the conduct of cases, are treated with scant courtesy by the presiding magistrate and are lucky if they get off with nothing worse. The majority of commercial cases come before the guilds, and are settled without reference to the authorities. The ordinary Chinese dread a court of justice, as a place in which both parties manage to lose something. "It is not the big devil," according to the current saying, "but the little devils" who frighten the suitor away. This is because official servants receive no salary, but depend for their livelihood on perquisites and tips; and the Chinese suitor, who is a party to the system, readily admits that it is necessary "to sprinkle a little water."

Neither do any officials in China, high or low, receive salaries, although absurdly inadequate sums are allocated by the Government for that purpose, for which it is considered prudent not to apply. The Chinese system is to some extent the reverse of our own. Our officials collect money and pay it into the Treasury, from which source fixed sums are returned to them as salaries. In China, the occupants of petty posts collect revenue in various ways, as taxes or fees, pay themselves as much as they dare, and hand up the balance to a superior officer, who in turn pays himself in the same sense, and again hands up the balance to his superior officer. When the viceroy of a province is reached, he too keeps what he dares, sending up to the Imperial exchequer in Peking just enough to satisfy the powers above him. There is thus a continual check by the higher grade upon the lower, but no check on such extortion as might be practiced upon the tax-payer. The tax-payer sees to that himself. Speaking generally, it may be said that this system, in spite of its unsatisfactory character, works fairly well. Few officials overstep the limits which custom has assigned to their posts, and those who do generally come to grief. So that when the dishonesty of the Chinese officials is held up to reprobation, it should always be remembered that the financial side of their public service is not surrounded with such formalities and safeguards as to make robbery of public money difficult, if not almost impossible. It is, therefore, all the more cheering when we find, as is frequently the case, retiring or transferred mandarins followed by the good wishes and affection of the people over whom they have been set to rule.

Until quite recently, there has been no such thing in China as municipal administration and rating, and even now such methods are only being tentatively introduced in large cities where there are a number of foreign residents. Occupants of houses are popularly supposed to "sweep the snow from their own doorsteps," but the repair of roads, bridges, drains, etc., has always been left to the casual philanthropy of wealthy individuals, who take these opportunities of satisfying public opinion in regard to the obligations of the rich towards the poor. Consequently, Chinese cities are left without efficient lighting, draining, or scavengering; and it is astonishing how good the health of the people living under these conditions can be. There is no organized police force; but cities are divided into wards, and at certain points barriers are drawn across the streets at night, with perhaps one watchman to each. It is not considered respectable to be out late at night, and it is not safe to move about without a lantern, which is carried, for those who can afford the luxury, by a servant preceding them.

One difference between life in China and life in this country may be illustrated to a certain extent in the following way. Supposing a traveler, passing through an English village, to be hit on the head by a stone. Unless he can point out his assailant, the matter is at an end. In China, all the injured party has to do is to point out the village—or, if a town, the ward—in which he was assaulted. Then the headman of such town or ward is summoned before the authorities and fined, proportionately to the offence, for allowing rowdy behavior in his district. The headman takes good care that he does not pay the fine himself. In the same way, parents are held responsible for the acts of their children, and householders for those of their servants.

CHAPTER III

RELIGION AND SUPERSTITION

The Chinese are emphatically not a religious people, though they are very superstitious. Belief in a God has come down from the remotest ages, but the old simple creed has been so overlaid by Buddhism as not to be discernible at the present day. Buddhism is now the dominant religion of China. It is closely bound up with the lives of the people, and is a never-failing refuge in sickness or worldly trouble. It is no longer the subtle doctrine which was originally presented to the people of India, but something much more clearly defined and appreciable by the plainest intellect. Buddha is the savior of the people through righteousness alone, and Buddhist saints are popularly supposed to possess intercessory powers. Yet reverence is always wanting; and crowds will laugh and talk, and buy and sell sweetmeats, in a Buddhist temple, before the very eyes of the most sacred images. So long as divine intervention is not required, an ordinary Chinaman is content to neglect his divinities; but no sooner does sickness or financial trouble come upon the family, than he will hurry off to propitiate the gods.

He accomplishes this through the aid of the priests, who receive his offerings of money, and light candles or incense at the shrine of the deity to be invoked. Buddhist priests are not popular with the Chinese, who make fun of their shaven heads, and doubt the sincerity of their convictions as well as the purity of their lives. "No meat nor wine may enter here" is a legend inscribed at the gate of most

Buddhist temples, the ordinary diet as served in the refectory being strictly vegetarian. A tipsy priest, however, is not an altogether unheard-of combination, and has provided more than one eminent artist with a subject of an interesting picture.

Yet the ordeal through which a novice must pass before being admitted to holy orders is a severe tax upon nerve and endurance. In the process of a long ritual, at least three, or even so many as nine, pastilles are placed upon the bald scalp of the head. These are then lighted, and allowed to burn down into the skin until permanent scars have been formed, the unfortunate novice being supported on both sides by priests who encourage him all the time to bear what must be excruciating pain. The fully qualified priest receives a diploma, on the strength of which he may demand a day and a night's board and lodging from the priests of any temple all over the empire.

At a very early date Buddhism had already taken a firm hold on the imagination of Chinese poets and painters, the latter of whom loved to portray the World-honored One in a dazzling hue of gold. A poet of the eighth century A.D., who realized for the first time the inward meaning of the Law, as it is called, ended a panegyric on Buddhism with the following lines:—

O thou pure Faith, had I but known thy scope,
The Golden God had long since been my hope!

Taoism is a term often met with in books about China. We are told that the three religions of the people are Confucianism, Buddhism, and Taoism, this being the order of precedence assigned to them in A.D. 568. Confucianism is of course not a religion at all, dealing as it does with duty towards one's neighbor and the affairs of this life only; and it will be seen that Taoism, in its true sense, has scarcely a stronger claim. At a very remote day, some say a thousand, and others six hundred, years before the Christian era, there flourished a wise man named Lao Tzu, which may be approximately pronounced as *Loudza* (*ou* as in *loud*), and understood to mean the Old Philosopher. He was a very original thinker, and a number of his sayings have been preserved to us by ancient authors, whom they had reached by tradition; that is to say, the Old Philosopher never put his doctrines into book form. There is indeed in existence a work which passes under his name, but it is now known to be a forgery, and is generally discarded by scholars.

The great flaw in the teaching of the Old Philosopher was its extremely impractical character, its unsuitability to the needs of men and women engaged in the ordinary avocations of life. In one sense he was an Anarchist, for he held that the empire would fare better if there were no government at all, the fact being that violence and disorder had always been conspicuous even under the best rulers. Similarly, he argued that we should get along more profitably with less learning, because then there would be fewer thieves, successful thieving being the result of mental training. It is not necessary to follow him to his most famous doctrine, namely, that of doing nothing, by which means, he declared, everything could be done, the solution of which puzzle of left everybody to find out for himself. Among his quaint sayings will be found several maxims of a very different class, as witness his injunction, "Requite evil with kindness," and "Mighty is he who conquers himself." Of the latter, the following illustration is given by a commentator. Two men meeting in the street, one said to the other, "How fat you have grown!" "Yes," replied his friend, "I have lately won a battle." "What do you mean?" inquired the former. "Why, you see," said the latter, "so long as I was at home, reading about ancient kings, I admired nothing but virtue; then, when I went out of doors, I was attracted by the charms of wealth and power. These two feelings fought inside me, and I began to lose flesh; but now love of virtue has conquered, and I am fat."

The teachings of the Old Philosopher were summed up in the word *Tao*, pronounced as *tou(t)*, which originally meant a road, a way; and as applied to doctrines means simply the right way or path of moral conduct, in which mankind should tread so as to lead correct and virtuous lives. Later on, when Buddhism was introduced, this Taoism, with all its paradoxes and subtleties, to which alchemy and the concoction of an elixir of life had been added, gradually began to lose its hold upon the people; and in order to stem the tide of opposition, temples and monasteries were built, a priesthood was established in imitation of the Buddhists, and all kinds of ceremonies and observances were taken from Buddhism, until, at the present day, only those who know can tell one from the other.

Although alchemy, which was introduced from Greece, via Bactria, in the second century B.C., has long ceased to interest the Chinese public, who have found out that gold is more easily made from the sweat of the brow than from copper or lead; and although only a few silly people now believe that any mixture of drugs will produce an elixir of life, able to confer immortality upon those who drink it; nevertheless, Taoism still professes to teach the art of extending life, if not indefinitely, at any rate to a considerable length. This art would probably go some way towards extending life under any circumstances, for it consists chiefly in deep and regular breathing, preferably of morning air, in swallowing the saliva three times in every two hours, in adopting certain positions for the body and limbs, which are also strengthened by gymnastic exercises, and finally, as borrowed from the Buddhists, in remaining motionless for some hours a day, the eyes shut, and the mind abstracted as much as possible from all surrounding influences. The upshot of these and other practices is the development of "the pure man," on which Chuang Tzu (*Chwongdza*), a Taoist philosopher of the third and fourth centuries B.C., to be mentioned again, writes as follows: "But what is a pure man? The pure men of old acted without calculation, not seeking to secure results. They laid no plans. Therefore, failing, they had no cause for regret; succeeding, no cause for congratulation. And thus they could scale heights without fear; enter water without becoming wet, and fire without feeling hot. The pure men of old slept without dreams, and waked without anxiety. They ate without discrimination, breathing deep breaths. For pure men draw breath from their heels; the vulgar only from their throats."

Coupled with what may be called intellectual Taoism, as opposed to the grosser form under which this faith appeals to the people at large, is a curious theory that human life reaches the earth from some extraordinarily dazzling centre away in the depths of space, "beyond the range of conceptions." This centre appears to be the home of eternal principles, the abode of a First Cause, where perfectly spotless and pure beings "drink of the spiritual and feed on force," and where likeness exists without form. To get back to that state should be the object of all men, and this is only to be attained by a process of mental and physical purification prolonged through all conditions of existence. Then, when body and soul are fitted for the change, there comes what ordinary mortals call death; and the pure being closes his eyes, to awake forthwith in his original glory from the sleep which mortals call life.

For many centuries Buddhism and Taoism were in bitter antagonism. Sometimes the court was Buddhist, sometimes Taoist; first one faith was suppressed altogether, then the other; in A.D. 574 both were abolished in deference to Confucianism, which, however, no emperor has ever dared to interfere with seriously. At present, all the "three religions" flourish happily side by side.

The Chinese believe firmly in the existence of spirits, which they classify simply as good and evil. They do not trouble their heads much about the former, but they are terribly afraid of the latter. Hideous devils infest dark corners, and lie in wait to injure unfortunate passers-by, often for no cause whatever. The spirits of persons who have been wronged are especially dreaded by those who have done the wrong. A man who has been defrauded of money will commit suicide, usually by poison, at the door of the wrongdoer, who will thereby first fall into the hands of the authorities, and if he escapes in that quarter, will still have to count with the injured ghost of his victim. A daughter-in-law will drown or hang herself to get free from, and also to avenge, the tyranny or cruelty of her husband's mother. These acts lead at once to family feuds, which sometimes end in bloodshed; more often in money compensation; and the known risk of such contingencies operates as a wholesome check upon aggressive treatment of the weak by the strong.

Divination and fortune-telling have always played a conspicuous part in ordinary Chinese life. Wise men, of the magician type, sit at stalls in street and market-place, ready for a small fee to advise those who consult them on any enterprise to be undertaken, even of the most trivial kind. The omens can be taken in various ways, as by calculation based upon books, of which there is quite a literature, or by drawing lots inscribed with mystic signs, to be interpreted by the fortune-teller. Even at Buddhist temples may be found two kidney-shaped pieces of wood, flat on one side and round on the other, which are thrown into the air before an altar, the results—two flats, two rounds, or one of each—being interpreted as unfavorable, medium, and very favorable, respectively.

Of all Chinese superstitions, the one that has been most persistent, and has exerted the greatest influence upon national life, is the famous Wind-and-Water system (*feng shui*) of geomancy. According to the principles which govern this system, and of which quite a special literature exists, the good or evil fortunes of individuals and the communities are determined by the various physical aspects and conditions which surround their everyday life. The shapes of hills, the presence or absence of water, the position of trees, the height of buildings, and so forth, are all matters of deep consideration to the professors of the geomantic art, who thrive on the ignorance of superstitious clients. They are called in to select propitious sites for houses and graves; and it often happens that if the fortunes of a family are failing, a geomancer will be invited to modify in some way the arrangement of the ancestral graveyard. Houses in a Chinese street are never built up so as to form a line of uniform height; every now and again one house must be a little higher or a little lower than its neighbor, or calamity will certainly ensue. It is impossible to walk straight into an ordinary middle-class dwelling-house. Just inside the front door there will be a fixed screen, which forces the visitor to turn to the right or to the left; the avowed object being to exclude evil spirits, which can only move in straight lines.

Mention of the ancestral graveyard brings to mind the universal worship of ancestors, which has been from time immemorial such a marked feature of Chinese religious life. At death, the spirit of a man or woman is believed to remain watching over the material interests of the family to which the deceased had belonged. Offerings of various kinds, including meat and drink, are from time to time made to such a spirit, supposed to be particularly resident in an ancestral hall—or cupboard, as the case may be. These offerings are made for the special purpose of conciliating the spirit, and of obtaining in return a liberal share of the blessings and good things of this life. This is the essential feature of the rite, and this it is which makes the rite an act of worship pure and simple; so that only superficial observers could make the mistake of classifying ancestral worship, as practiced in China, with such acts as laying wreaths upon the tombs of deceased friends and relatives.

With reference to the spirit or soul, the Chinese have held for centuries past that the soul of every man is twofold; in a popular acceptation it is sometimes regarded as threefold. One portion is that which expresses the visible personality, and is permanently attached to the body; the other has the power of leaving the body, carrying with it an appearance of physical form, which accounts for a person being seen in two different places at once. Cases of catalepsy or trance are explained by the Chinese as the absence from the body of this portion of the soul, which is also believed to be expelled from the body by any violent shock or fright. There is a story of a man who was so terrified at the prospect of immediate execution that his separable soul left his body, and he found himself sitting on the eaves of a house, from which point he could see a man bound, and waiting for the executioner's sword. Just then, a reprieve arrived, and in a moment he was back again in his body. Mr. Edmund Gosse, who can hardly have been acquainted with the Chinese view, told a similar story in his *Father and Son*: "During morning and evening prayers, which were extremely lengthy and fatiguing, I fancied that one of my two selves could flit up, and sit clinging to the cornice, and look down on my other self and the rest of us."

In some parts of China, planchette is frequently resorted to as a means of reading the future, and adapting one's actions accordingly. It is a purely professional performance, being carried through publicly before some altar in a temple, and payment made for the response. The question is written down on a piece of paper, which is burnt at the altar apparently before any one could gather knowledge of its contents; and the answer from the god is forthwith traced on a tray of sand, word by word, each word being obliterated to make room for the next, by two men, supposed to be ignorant of the question, who hold the ends of a V-shaped instrument from the point of which a little wooden pencil projects at right angles.

Another method of extracting information from the spirits of the unseen world is nothing more or less than hypnotism, which has long been known to the Chinese, and is mentioned in literature so far back as the middle of the seventeenth century. With all the paraphernalia of altar, candles, incense, etc., a medium is thrown into a hypnotic condition, during which his body is supposed to be possessed by a spirit, and every word he may utter to be divinely inspired. An amusing instance is recorded of a medium who, while under hypnotic influence, not only blurted out the pecuniary defalcations of certain men who had been collecting in aid of temple restoration, but went so far as to admit that he had had some of the money himself.

This same influence is also used in cases of serious illness, but always secretly, for such practices, as well as dark *seances* for communicating with spirits, are strictly forbidden by the Chinese authorities, who regard the employment of occult means as more likely to be subversive of morality than to do any good whatever to a sick person, or to any one else. All secret societies of any sort or kind are equally under the ban of the law, the assumption—a very justifiable one—being that the aim of these societies is to upset the existing order of political and social life. The Heaven-and-Earth Society is among the most famous, and the most dreaded, partly perhaps because it has never been entirely suppressed. The lodges of this fraternity, the oath of fidelity, and the ceremonial of admission, remind one forcibly of Masonry in the West; but the points of conduct are merely coincidences, and there does not appear to be any real connection.

Among the most curious of all these institutions is the Golden Orchid Society, the girl-members of which swear never to marry, and not only threaten, but positively commit suicide upon any attempt at coercion. At one time this society became such a serious menace that the authorities were compelled to adopt severe measures of repression.

Another old-established society is that of the Vegetarians, who eat no meat and neither smoke nor drink. From their seemingly harmless ranks it is said that the Boxers of 1900 were largely recruited.

For nearly twenty-five centuries the Chinese have looked to Confucius for their morals. Various religions have appealed to the spiritual side of the Chinese mind, and Buddhism has obtained an ascendancy which will not be easily displaced; but through all this long lapse of time the morality of China has been under the guidance of their great teacher, Confucius (551-479 B.C.), affectionately known to them as the "uncrowned king," and recently raised to the rank of a god.

His doctrines, in the form sometimes of maxims, sometimes of answers to eager inquirers, were brought together after his death—we do not know exactly how soon—and have influenced first and last an enormous proportion of the human race. Confucius taught man's duty to his neighbor; he taught virtue for virtue's sake, and not for the hope of reward or fear of punishment; he taught loyalty to the sovereign as the foundation stone of national prosperity, and filial piety as the basis of all happiness in the life of the people. As a simple human moralist he saw clearly the limitations of humanity, and refused to teach his disciples to return good for evil, as suggested by the Old Philosopher, declaring without hesitation that evil should be met by justice. The first systematic writer of Chinese history, who died about 80 B.C., expressed himself on the position and influence of Confucius in terms which have been accepted as accurate for twenty centuries past: "Countless are the princes and prophets that the world has seen in its time—glorious in life, forgotten in death. But Confucius, though only a humble member of the cotton-clothed masses, remains with us after numerous generations. He is the model for such as would be wise. By all, from the Son of Heaven down to the meanest student, the supremacy of his principles is freely and fully admitted. He may indeed be pronounced the divinest of men."

The Son of Heaven is of course the Emperor, who is supposed to be God's chosen representative on earth, and responsible for the right conduct and well-being of all committed to his care. Once every year he proceeds in state to the Temple of Heaven at Peking; and after the due performance of sacrificial worship he enters alone the central raised building with circular blue-tiled roof, and there places himself in communication with the Supreme Being, submitting for approval or otherwise his stewardship during the preceding twelve months. Chinese records go so far as to mention letters received from God. There is a legend of the sixth century A.D., which claims that God revealed Himself to a hermit in a retired valley, and bestowed on him a tablet of jade with a mysterious inscription. But there is a much more circumstantial account of a written communication which in A.D. 1008 descended from heaven upon mount T'ai, the famous mountain in Shantung, where a temple has been built to mark the very spot. The emperor and his courtiers regarded this letter with profound reverence and awe, which roused the ire of a learned statesman of the day. The latter pointed out that Confucius, when asked to speak, so that his disciples might have something to record, had bluntly replied: "Does God speak? The four seasons pursue their courses and all things are produced; but does God say anything?" Therefore, he argued, if God does not speak to us, still less will He write a letter.

The fact that the receipt of such a letter is mentioned in the dynastic history of the period must not be allowed to discredit in any way the general truth and accuracy of Chinese annals, which, as research progresses, are daily found to be far more trustworthy than was ever expected to be the case. We ourselves do not wholly reject the old contemporary chronicles of Hoveden and Roger of Wendover because they mention a letter from Christ on the neglect of the Sabbath.

In Chinese life, social and political alike, filial piety may be regarded as the keystone of the arch. Take that away, and the superstructure of centuries crumbles to the ground. When Confucius was asked by one of his disciples to explain what constituted filial piety, he replied that it was a difficult obligation to define; while to another disciple he was able to say without hesitation that the mere support of parents would be insufficient, inasmuch as food is what is supplied even to horses and dogs. According to the story-books for children, the obligation has been interpreted by the people at large in many different ways. The twenty-four standard examples of filial children include a son who allowed mosquitoes to feed upon him, and did not drive them away lest they should go and annoy his parents; another son who wept so passionately because he could procure no bamboo shoots for his mother that the gods were touched, and up out of the ground came some shoots which he gathered and carried home; another who when carrying buckets of water would slip and fall on purpose, in order to make his parents laugh; and so on. No wonder that Confucius found filial piety beyond his powers of definition.

Now for a genuine example. There is a very wonderful novel in which a very affecting love-story is worked out to a terribly tragic conclusion. The heroine, a beautiful and fascinating girl, finally dies of consumption, and the hero, a wayward but none the less fascinating youth, enters the Buddhist priesthood. A lady, the mother of a clever young official, was so distressed by the pathos of the tale that she became quite ill, and doctors prescribed medicines in vain. At length, when things were becoming serious, the son set to work and composed a sequel to this novel, in which he resuscitated the heroine and made the lovers happy by marriage; and in a short time he had the intense satisfaction of seeing his mother restored to health.

Other forms of filial piety, which bear no relation whatever to the fanciful fables given above, are commonly practiced by all classes. In consequence of the serious or prolonged illness of parents, it is very usual for sons and daughters to repair to the municipal temple and pray that a certain number of years may be cut off their own span of life and added to that of the sick parents in question.

Let us now pause to take stock of some of the results which have accrued from the operation and influence of Confucianism during such a long period, and over such swarming myriads of the human race. It is a commonplace in the present day to assert that the Chinese are hardworking, thrifty, and sober—the last-mentioned, by the way, in a land where drunkenness is not regarded as a crime. Shallow observers of the globe-trotter type, who have had their pockets picked by professional thieves in Hong-Kong, and even resident observers who have not much cultivated their powers of observation and comparison, will assert that honesty is a virtue denied to the Chinese; but those who have lived long in China and have more seriously devoted themselves to discover the truth, may one and all be said to be arrayed upon the other side. The amount of solid honesty to be met with in every class, except the professionally criminal class, is simply astonishing. That the word of the Chinese merchant is as good as his bond has long since become a household word, and so it is in other walks of life. With servants from respectable families, the householder need have no fear for his goods. "Be loyal," says the native maxim, "to the master whose rice you eat;" and this maxim is usually fulfilled to the letter. Hence, it is that many foreigners who have been successful in their business careers, take care to see, on their final departure from the East, that the old and faithful servant, often of twenty to thirty years' standing, shall have some provision for himself and his family. In large establishments, especially banks, in which great interests are at stake, it is customary for the Chinese staff to be guaranteed by some wealthy man (or firm), who deposits securities for a considerable amount, thus placing the employer in a very favorable position. The properly chosen Chinese servant who enters the household of a foreigner, is a being to whom, as suggested above, his master often becomes deeply attached, and whom he parts with, often after many years of service, to his everlasting regret. Such a servant has many virtues. He is noiseless over his work, which he performs efficiently. He can stay up late, and yet rise early. He lives on the establishment, but in an out-building. He provides his own food. He rarely wants to absent himself, and even then will always provide a reliable *locum tenens*. He studies his master's ways, and learns to anticipate his slightest wishes. In return for these and other services he expects to get his wages punctually paid, and to be allowed to charge, without any notice being taken of the same, a commission on all purchases. This is the Chinese system, and even a servant absolutely honest in any other way cannot emancipate himself from its grip. But if treated fairly, he will not abuse his chance. One curious feature of the system is that if one master is in a relatively higher position than another, the former will be charged by his servants slightly more than the latter by his servants for precisely the same article. Many attempts have been made by foreigners to break through this "old custom," especially by offering higher wages; but signal failure has always been the result, and those masters have invariably succeeded best who have fallen in with the existing institution, and have tried to make the best of it.

There is one more, and in many ways the most important, side of a Chinese servant's character. He will recognize frankly, and without a pang, the superior position and the rights of his master; but at the same time, if worth keeping, he will exact from his master the proper respect due from man to man. It is wholly beside the mark to say that he will not put up for a moment with the cuffs and kicks so freely administered to his Indian colleague. A respectable Chinese servant will often refuse to remain with a master who uses abusive or violent language, or shows signs of uncontrollable temper. A lucrative place is as nothing compared with the "loss of face" which he would suffer in the eyes of his friends; in other words, with his loss of dignity as a man. If a servant will put up with a blow, the best course is to dismiss him at once, as worthless and unreliable, if not actually dangerous. Confucius said: "If you mistrust a man, do not employ him; if you employ a man, do not mistrust him;" and this will still be found to be an excellent working rule in dealings with Chinese servants.

CHAPTER IV

A.D. 220-1200

The long-lived and glorious House of Han was brought to a close by the usual causes. There were palace intrigues and a temporary usurpation of the throne, eunuchs of course being in the thick of the mischief; added to which a very serious rebellion broke out, almost as a natural consequence. First and last there arose three aspirants to the Imperial yellow, which takes the place of purple in ancient Rome; the result being that, after some years of hard fighting, China was divided into three parts, each ruled by one of the three rivals. The period is known in history as that of the Three Kingdoms, and lasted from A.D. 220 to A.D. 265. This short space of time was filled, especially the early years, with stirring deeds of heroism and marvelous strategical operations, fortune favoring first one of the three commanders and then another. The whole story of these civil wars is most graphically told in a famous historical romance composed about a thousand years afterwards. As in the case of the Waverley novels, a considerable amount of fiction has been interwoven with truth to make the narrative more palatable to the general reader; but its basis is history, and the work is universally regarded among the Chinese themselves as one of the most valuable productions in the lighter branches of their literature.

The three to four centuries which follow on the above period were a time of political and social disorganization, unfavorable, according to Chinese writers, to the development of both literature and art. The House of Chin, which at first held sway over a once more united empire, was severely harassed by the Tartars on the north, who were in turn overwhelmed by the House of Toba. The latter ruled for some two hundred years over northern China, while the southern portions were governed by several short-lived native dynasties. A few points in connection with these times deserve perhaps brief mention.

The old rule of twenty-seven months of mourning for parents was re-established, and has continued in force down to the present day. The Japanese sent occasional missions, with tribute; and the Chinese, who had already in A.D. 240 dispatched an envoy to Japan, repeated the compliment in 608. An attempt was made to conquer Korea, and envoys were sent to countries as far off as Siam. Buddhism, which had been introduced many centuries previously—no one can exactly say when—began to spread far and wide, and appeared to be firmly established. In A.D. 399 a Buddhist priest, named Fa Hsien, started from Central China and travelled to India across the great desert and over the Hindu Kush, subsequently visiting Patna, Benares, Buddha-Gaya, and other well-known spots, which he accurately described in the record of his journey published on his return and still in existence. His object was to obtain copies of the sacred books, relics and images, illustrative of the faith; and these he safely conveyed to China by sea from India, via Ceylon (where he spent three years), and Sumatra, arriving after an absence of fifteen years.

In the year A.D. 618 the House of T'ang entered upon its glorious course of three centuries in duration. Under a strong but dissolute ruler immediately preceding, China had once more become a united empire, undivided against itself; and although wars and rebellions were not wanting to disturb the even tenor of its way, the general picture presented to us under the new dynasty of the T'angs is one of national peace, prosperity, and progress. The name of this House has endured, like that of Han, to the present day in the popular language of the people; for just as the northerners still delight to style themselves "good sons of Han," so are the southerners still proud to speak of themselves as "men of T'ang."

One of the chief political events of this period was the usurpation of power by the Empress Wu—at first, as nominal regent on behalf of a step-child, the son and heir of her late husband by his first wife, and afterwards, when she had set aside the step-child, on her own account. There had been one previous instance of a woman wielding the Imperial scepter, namely, the Empress Lu of the Han dynasty, to whom the Chinese have accorded the title of legitimate ruler, which has not been allowed to the Empress Wu. The latter, however, was possessed of much actual ability, mixed with a kind of midsummer madness; and so long as her great intellectual faculties remained unimpaired, she ruled, like her successor of some twelve centuries afterwards, with a rod of iron. In her old age she was deposed and dismissed to private life, the rightful heir being replaced upon his father's throne.

Among the more extravagant acts of her reign are some which are still familiar to the people of to-day. Always, even while her husband was alive, she was present, behind a curtain, at councils and audiences; after his death she was accustomed to take her place openly among the ministers of state, wearing a false beard. In 694 she gave herself the title of Divine Empress, and in 696 she even went so far as to style herself God Almighty. In her later years she became hopelessly arrogant and overbearing. No one was allowed to say that the Empress was fair as a lily or lovely as a rose, but that the lily was fair or the rose lovely as Her Majesty. She tried to spread the belief that she was really the Supreme Being by forcing flowers artificially and then in the presence of her courtiers ordering them to bloom. On one occasion she commanded some peonies to bloom; and because they did not instantly obey, she caused every peony in the capital to be pulled up and burnt, and prohibited the cultivation of peonies ever afterwards. She further decided to place her sex once and for all on an equality with man. For that purpose women were admitted to the public examinations, official posts being conferred upon those who were successful; and among other things they were excused from kneeling while giving evidence in courts of justice. This innovation, however, did not fulfill its promise; and with the disappearance of its vigorous founders, the system also disappeared. It was not actually the first time in Chinese history that the experiment had been tried. An emperor of the third century A.D. had already opened public life to women, and it is said that many of them rose to high office; but here too the system was of short duration, and the old order was soon restored.

Another striking picture of the T'ang dynasty is presented by the career of an emperor who is usually spoken of as Ming Huang, and who, after distinguishing himself at several critical junctures, mounted the throne in 712, in succession to his father, who had abdicated in his favor. He began with economy, closing the silk factories and forbidding the palace ladies to wear jewels or embroideries, considerable quantities of which were actually burnt. He was a warm patron of literature, and schools were established in every village. Fond of music, he founded a college for training youth of both sexes in this art. His love of war and his growing extravagance led to increased taxation, with the usual consequences in China—discontent and rebellion. He surrounded himself by a brilliant court, welcoming men of genius in literature and art; at first for their talents alone, but finally for their readiness to participate in scenes of revelry and dissipation provided for the amusement of a favorite concubine, the ever-famous Yang Kuei-fei (pronounced *Kway-fay*). Eunuchs were appointed to official posts, and the grossest forms of religious superstition were encouraged. Women ceased to veil themselves, as of old. At length, in 755, a serious rebellion broke out, and a year later the emperor, now an old man of seventy-one, fled before the storm. He had not proceeded far before his soldiery revolted and demanded vengeance upon the whole family of the favorite, several unworthy members of which had been raised to high positions and loaded with honors. The wretched emperor was forced to order the head eunuch to strangle his idolized concubine, while the rest of her family perished at the hands of the troops. He subsequently abdicated in favor of his son, and spent the last six years of his life in seclusion.

This tragic story has been exquisitely told in verse by one of China's foremost poets, who was born only a few years later. He divides his poem into eight parts, dealing with the *ennui* of the monarch until he discovers *beauty*, the *revelry* of the pair together, followed by the horrors of *flight*, to end in the misery of *exile* without her, the *return* when the emperor passes again by the fatal spot, *home* where everything reminds him of her, and finally *spirit-land*. This last is a figment of the poet's imagination. He pictures the disconsolate emperor sending a magician to discover Yang Kuei-fei's whereabouts in the next world, and to bear to her a message of uninterrupted love. The magician, after a long search, finds her in one of the Isles of the Blest, and fulfils his commission accordingly.

> Her features are fixed and calm, though myriad tears fall,
> Wetting a spray of pear-bloom, as it were with the raindrops
>   of spring.
> Subduing her emotions, restraining her grief, she tenders
>   thanks to His Majesty.
> Saying how since their parting she had missed his form and
>   voice;
> And how, although their love on earth had so soon come to
>   an end,
> The days and months among the Blest were still of long
>   duration.
> And now she turns and gazes towards the above of mortals,
> But cannot discern the Imperial city, lost in the dust and
>   haze.
> Then she takes out the old keepsake, tokens of undying love,
> A gold hairpin, an enamel brooch, and bids the magician
>   carry these back.

One half of the hairpin she keeps, and one half of the enamel
    brooch,
Breaking with her hands the yellow gold, and dividing the
    enamel in two.
"Tell him," she said, "to be firm of heart, as this gold and
    enamel,
And then in heaven or on earth below we two may meet once
    more."

The magnificent House of T'ang was succeeded by five insignificant dynasties, the duration of all of which was crowded into about half a century. Then, in A.D. 960, began the rule of the Sungs (pronounced *Soongs*), to last for three hundred years and rival in national peace and prosperity any other period in the history of China. The nation had already in a great measure settled down to that state of material civilization and mental culture in which it has remained to the present time. To the appliances of ordinary Chinese life it is probable that but few additions have been made since a very early date. The dress of the people has indeed undergone several variations, but the ploughs and hoes, the water-wheels and well-sweeps, the tools of the artisans, mud huts, carts, junks, chairs, tables, chopsticks, etc., which we still see in China, are probably very much those of two thousand years ago. Mencius, of the third century B.C., observed that written characters had the same form, and axle-trees the same breadth, all over the empire; and to this day an unaltering uniformity is one of the chief characteristics of the Chinese people in every department of life.

In spite, however, of the peaceful aspirations of the House of Sung, the Kitan Tartars were for ever encroaching upon Chinese territory, and finally overran and occupied a large part of northern China, with their capital where Peking now stands. This resulted in an amicable arrangement to divide the empire, the Kitans retaining their conquests in the north, from which, after about two hundred years, they were in turn expelled by the Golden Tartars, who had previously been subject to them.

Many volumes, rather than pages, would be required to do justice to the statesmen, soldiers, philosophers, poets, historians, art critics, and other famous men of this dynasty. It has already been stated that the interpretation of the Confucian Canon, accepted at the present day, dates from this period; and it may now be of interest to give a brief account of another remarkable movement connected with the dynasty, though in quite a different line.

Wang An-shih (as *shi* in *shirk*), popularly known as the Reformer, was born in 1021. In his youth a keen student, his pen seemed to fly over the paper. He rose to high office; and by the time he was forty-eight he found himself installed as confidential adviser to the emperor. He then entered upon a series of startling political reforms, said to be based upon new and more correct interpretations of portions of the Confucian Canon, which still remained, so far as explanation was concerned, just as it had been left by the scholars of the Han dynasty. This appeal to authority was, of course, a mere blind, cleverly introduced to satisfy the bulk of the population, who were always unwilling to move in any direction where no precedent is forthcoming. One of his schemes, the express object of which was to decrease taxation and at the same time to increase the revenue, was to secure a sure and certain market for all products, as follows. From the produce of a given district, enough was to be set aside (1) for the payment of taxes, and (2) to supply the wants of the district; (3) the balance was then to be taken over by the state at a low rate, and held for a rise or forwarded to some centre where there happened to be a demand. There would be thus a certainty of market for the farmer, and an equal certainty for the state to make profits as a middleman. Another part of this scheme consisted in obligatory advances by the state to cultivators of land, whether these farmers required the money or not, the security for the loans being in each case the growing crops.

There was also a system of tithing for military purposes, under which every family having more than two males was bound to supply one to serve as a soldier; and in order to keep up a breed of cavalry horses, every family was compelled to take charge of one, which was provided, together with its food, by the government. There was a system under which money payments were substituted for the old-fashioned and vexatious method of carrying on public works by drafts of forced laborers; and again another under which warehouses for bartering and hypothecating goods were established all over the empire.

Of all his innovations the most interesting was that all land was to be remeasured and an attempt made to secure a more equitable incidence of taxation. The plan was to divide up the land into equal squares, and to levy taxes in proportion to the fertility of each. This scheme proved for various reasons to be unworkable; and the bitter opposition with which, like all his other measures of reform, it was received by his opponents, did not conduce to success. Finally, he abolished all restrictions upon the export of copper, the result being that even the current copper "cash" were melted down and made into articles for sale and exportation. A panic ensued, which Wang met by the simple expedient of doubling the value of each cash. He attempted to reform the examination system, requiring from the candidate not so much graces of style as a wide acquaintance with practical subjects. "Accordingly," says one Chinese author, "even the pupils at the village schools threw away their text-books of rhetoric, and began to study primers of history, geography, and political economy"—a striking anticipation of the movement in vogue to-day. "I have myself been," he tells us, "an omnivorous reader of books of all kinds, even, for example, of ancient medical and botanical works. I have, moreover, dipped into treatises on agriculture and on needlework, all of which I have found very profitable in aiding me to seize the great scheme of the Canon itself." But like many other great men, he was in advance of his age. He fell into disfavor at court, and was dismissed to a provincial post; and although he was soon recalled, he retired into private life, shortly afterwards to die, but not before he had seen the whole of his policy reversed.

His career stands out in marked contrast with that of the great statesman and philosopher, Chu Hsi (pronounced *Choo Shee*), who flourished A.D. 1130-1200. His literary output was enormous and his official career successful; but his chief title to fame rests upon his merits as a commentator on the Confucian Canon. As has been already stated, he introduced interpretations either wholly or partly at variance with those which had been put forth by the scholars of the Han dynasty, and hitherto received as infallible, thus modifying to a certain extent the prevailing standard of political and social morality. His guiding principle was merely one of consistency. He refused to interpret words in a given passage in one sense, and the same words occurring elsewhere in another sense. The effect of this apparently obvious method was magical; and from that date the teachings of Confucius have been universally understood in the way in which Chu Hsi said they ought to be understood.

To his influence also must be traced the spirit of materialism which is so widely spread among educated Chinese. The God in whom Confucius believed, but whom, as will be seen later on, he can scarcely be said to have "taught," was a passive rather than an active God, and may be compared with the God of the Psalms. He was a personal God, as we know from the ancient character by which He was designated in the written language of early ages, that character being a rude picture of a man. This view was entirely set aside by Chu Hsi, who declared in the plainest terms that the Chinese word for God meant nothing more than "abstract right;" in other words, God was a principle. It is impossible to admit such a proposition, which was based on sentiment and not on sound reasoning. Chu Hsi was emphatically not a man of religious temperament, and belief in the supernatural was distasteful to him; he was for a short time under the spell of Buddhism, but threw that religion over for the orthodoxy of Confucianism. He was, therefore, anxious to exclude the supernatural altogether from the revised scheme of moral conduct which he was deducing from the Confucian Canon, and his interpretation of the word "God" has been blindly accepted ever since.

When Chu Hsi died, his coffin is said to have taken up a position, suspended in the air, about three feet from the ground. Whereupon his son-in-law, falling on his knees beside the bier, reminded the departed spirit of the great principles of which he had been such a brilliant exponent in life—and the coffin descended gently to the ground.

CHAPTER V

WOMEN AND CHILDREN

The Chinese are very fond of animals, and especially of birds; and on the whole they may be said to be kind to their animals, though cases of ill-treatment occur. At the same time it must be carefully remembered that such quantum of humanity as they may exhibit is entirely of their own making; there is no law to act persuasively on brutal natures, and there is no Society for the Prevention of Cruelty to Animals to see that any such law is enforced. A very large number of beautiful birds, mostly songless, are found in various parts of China, and a great variety of fishes in the rivers and on the coast. Wild animals are represented by the tiger (in both north and south), the panther and the bear, and even the elephant and the rhinoceros may be found in the extreme south-west. The wolf and the fox, the latter dreaded as an uncanny beast, are very widely distributed.

Still less would there be any ground for establishing a Society for the Prevention of Cruelty to Children, the very name of which would make an ordinary, unsophisticated Chinaman stare. Chinese parents are, if anything, over-indulgent to their children. The father is, indeed, popularly known as the "Severe One," and it is a Confucian tradition that he should not spare the rod and so spoil the child, but he draws the line at a poker; and although as a father he possesses the power of life and death over his offspring, such punishments as are inflicted are usually of the mildest description. The

55

mother, the "Gentle One," is, speaking broadly, a soft-hearted, sweet-natured specimen of humanity; one of those women to whom hundreds of Europeans owe deep debts of gratitude for the care and affection lavished upon their alien children. In the absence of the Severe One, it falls to her to chastise when necessary; and we even read of a son who wept, not because his mother hurt him, but because, owing to her advanced age, she was no longer able to hit him hard enough!

Among other atrocious libels which have fastened upon the fair fame of the Chinese people, first and foremost stands the charge of female infanticide, now happily, though still slowly, fading from the calculations of those who seek the truth. Fifty years ago it was generally believed that the Chinese hated their female children, and got rid of them in early infancy by wholesale murder. It may be admitted at once that boys are preferred to girls, inasmuch as they carry on the family line, and see that the worship of ancestors is regularly performed in due season. Also, because girls require dowries, which they take away with them for the benefit of other families than their own; hence the saying, "There is no thief like a family of five daughters," and the term "lose-money goods," as jestingly applied to girls, against which may be set another term, "a thousand ounces of gold," which is commonly used of a daughter. Of course it is the boy who is specially wanted in a family; and little boys are often dressed as little girls, in order to deceive the angels of disease and death, who, it is hoped, may thus pass them over as of less account.

To return to the belief formerly held that female infanticide was rampant all over China. The next step was for the honest observer to admit that it was not known in his own particular district, but to declare that it was largely practiced elsewhere. This view, however, lost its validity when residents "elsewhere" had to allow that no traces of infanticide could be found in their neighborhood; and so on. Luckily, still greater comfort is to be found in the following argument,—a rare example of proving a negative—from which it will be readily seen that female infanticide on any abnormal scale is quite beyond the bounds of the possible. Those who have even a bowing acquaintance with Chinese social life will grant that every boy, at about the age of eighteen, is provided by his parents with a wife. They must also concede the notorious fact that many well-to-do Chinese take one or more concubines. The Emperor, indeed, is allowed seventy; but this number exists only on paper as a regulation maximum. Now, if every Chinaman has one wife, and many have two, over and above the host of girls said to be annually sacrificed as worthless babies, it must follow that the proportion of girls born in China enormously outnumbers the proportion of boys, whereas in the rest of the world boys are well known to be always in the majority. After this, it is perhaps superfluous to state that, apart from the natural love of the parent, a girl is really, even at a very early age, a marketable commodity. Girls are sometimes sold into other families to be brought up as wives for the sons; more often, to be used as servants, under what is of course a form of slavery, qualified by the important condition, which can be enforced by law, that when of a marriageable age, the girl's master shall find her a husband. Illegitimate children, the source of so much baby-farming and infanticide elsewhere, are practically unknown in China; and the same may be said of divorce. A woman cannot legally divorce her husband. In rare cases she will leave him, and return to her family, in spite of the fact that he can legally insist upon her return; for she knows well that if her case is good, the husband will not dare to risk the scandal of an exposure, not to mention the almost certain vengeance of her affronted kinsmen. It is also the fear of such vengeance that prevents mothers-in-law from ill-treating the girls who pass into their new homes rather as servants than daughters to the husband's mother. Every woman, as indeed every man, has one final appeal by which to punish an oppressor. She may commit suicide, there being no canon, legal or moral, against self-slaughter; and in China, where, contrary to widespread notions on the subject, human life is held in the highest degree sacred, this course is sure to entail trouble and expense, and possibly severe punishment, if the aggrieved parties are not promptly conciliated by a heavy money payment.

A man may divorce his wife for one of the seven following reasons:—Want of children, adultery, neglect of his parents, nagging, thieving (i.e. supplying her own family with his goods, popularly known as "leakage"), jealous temper and leprosy. To the above, the humanity of the lawgiver has affixed three qualifying conditions. He may not put her away on any of the above grounds if she has duly passed through the period of mourning for his parents; if he has grown rich since their marriage; if she has no longer any home to which she can return.

Altogether, the Chinese woman has by no means such a bad time as is generally supposed to be the case. Even in the eye of the law, she has this advantage over a man, that she cannot be imprisoned except for high treason and adultery, and is to all intents and purposes exempt from the punishment of the bamboo. Included in this exemption are the aged and the young, the sick, the hungry and naked, and those who have already suffered violence, as in a brawl. Further, in a well-known handbook, magistrates are advised to postpone, in certain circumstances, the infliction of corporal punishment; as for instance, when either the prisoner or they themselves may be under the influence of excitement, anger or drink.

The bamboo is the only instrument with which physical punishment may legally be inflicted; and its infliction on a prisoner or recalcitrant witness, in order to extort evidence, constitutes what has long been dignified as "torture;" but even that is now, under a changing system, about to disappear. This must not be taken to mean that torture, in our sense of the term, has never been applied in China. The real facts of the case are these. Torture, except as already described, being constitutionally illegal, no magistrate would venture to resort to it if there were any chance of his successful impeachment before the higher authorities, upon which he would be cashiered and his official career brought abruptly to an end. Torture, therefore, would have no terrors for the ordinary citizen of good repute and with a backing of substantial friends; but for the outcast, the rebel, the highway robber (against whom every man's hand would be), the disreputable native of a distant province, and also for the outer barbarian (e.g. the captives at the Summer Palace in 1860), another tale must be told. No consequences, except perhaps promotion, would follow from too rigorous treatment in such cases as these.

Resort to the bamboo as a means of extorting the confession of a prisoner is regarded by the people rather as the magistrate's confession of his own incapacity. The education of the official, too easily and too freely turned into ridicule, gives him an insight into human nature which, coupled with a little experience, renders him extremely formidable to the shifty criminal or the crafty litigant. As a rule, he finds no need for the application of pain. There is a quaint story illustrative of such judicial methods as would be sure to meet with full approbation in China. A magistrate, who after several hearings had failed to discover, among a gang accused of murder, what was essential to the completion of the case, namely, the actual hand which struck the fatal blow, notified the prisoners that he was about to invoke the assistance of the spirits, with a view to elicit the truth. Accordingly, he caused the accused men, dressed in the black clothes of criminals, to be led into a large barn, and arranged around it, face to the wall. Having then told them that an accusing angel would shortly come among them, and mark the back of the guilty man, he went outside and had the door shut, and the place darkened. After a short interval, when the door was thrown open, and the men were summoned to come forth, it was seen directly that one of the number had a white mark on his back. This man, in order to make all secure, had turned his back to the wall, not knowing, what the magistrate well knew, that the wall had been newly white-washed.

As to the punishment of crime by flogging, a sentence of one or two hundred—even more—blows would seem to be cruel and disgusting; happily, it may be taken for granted that such ferocious sentences are executed only in such cases as have been mentioned above. An acute observer, for many years a member of the municipal police force in Shanghai, whose duty it was to see that floggings were administered to Chinese criminals, stated plainly in a public report that the bamboo is not necessarily a severe ordeal, and that one hundred blows are at times inflicted so lightly as to leave scarcely a mark behind, though the recipient howls loudly all the time. Those criminals who have money can always manage to square the gaoler; and the gaoler has acquired a certain knack in laying on, the upshot being great cry and little wool, very satisfactory to the culprit. Even were we to accept the cruelest estimate in regard to punishment by the bamboo, it would only go to show that humanitarian feelings in China are lagging somewhat behind our own. In *The Times* of March 1, 1811, we read that, for allowing French prisoners to escape from Dartmoor, three men of the Nottingham militia were sentenced to receive 900 lashes each, and that one of them actually received 450 lashes in the presence of pickets from every regiment in the garrison. On New Year's Day, 1911, a eunuch attempted to assassinate one of the Imperial Princes. For this he was sentenced to be beaten to death, some such ferocious punishment being necessary, in Chinese eyes, to vindicate the majesty of the law. That end having been attained, the sentence was commuted to eighty blows with the bamboo and deportation to northern Manchuria.

The Chinese woman often, in mature life, wields enormous influence over the family, males included, and is a kind of private Empress Dowager. A man knows, says the proverb, but a woman knows better. As a widow in early life, her lot is not quite so pleasant. It is not thought desirable for widows to remarry; but if she remains single, she becomes "a rudderless boat;" round which gathers much calumny. Many young women brave public opinion, and enter into second nuptials. If they are bent upon remarrying, runs the saying, they can no more be prevented than the sky can be prevented from raining.

The days of "golden lilies," as the artificially small feet of Chinese women are called, are generally believed to date from the tenth century A.D., though some writers have endeavoured to place the custom many centuries earlier. It must always be carefully remembered that Manchu women—the women of the dynasty which has ruled since 1644—do not compress their feet. Consequently, the empresses of modern times have feet of the natural size; neither is the practice in force among the Hakkas, a race said to have migrated from the north of China to the south in the thirteenth century; nor among the hill tribes; nor among the boating population of Canton and elsewhere. Small feet are thus in no way associated with aristocracy or gentleness of birth; neither is there any foundation for the generally received opinion that the Chinese lame their women in this way to keep them from gadding about. Small-footed women may be seen carrying quite heavy burdens, and even working in the fields; not to mention that many are employed as nurses for small children. Another explanation is that women with bound feet bear finer children and stronger; but the real reason lies in another direction, quite beyond the scope of this book. The question of charm may be taken into consideration, for any Chinaman will bear witness to the seductive effect of a gaily-dressed girl picking her way on tiny feet some three inches in length, her swaying movements and delightful appearance of instability conveying a general sense of delicate grace quite beyond expression in words.

The lady of the tenth century, to whom the origin of small feet is ascribed, wished to make her own feet like two new moons; but whether she actually bound them, as at the present day, is purely a matter of conjecture. The modern style of binding inflicts great pain for a long time upon the little girls who have to endure it. They become very shy on the subject, and will on no account show their bare feet, though Manchu women and others with full-sized feet frequently walk about unshod, and the boat-girls at Canton and elsewhere never seem to wear shoes or stockings at all.

The "pigtail," or long plait of hair worn by all Chinamen, for the abolition of which many advanced reformers are now earnestly pleading, is an institution of comparatively modern date. It was imposed by the victorious Manchu-Tartars when they finally established their dynasty in 1644, not so much as a badge of conquest, still less of servitude, but as a means of obliterating, so far as possible, the most patent distinction between the two races, and of unifying the appearance, if not the aspirations, of the subjects of the Son of Heaven. This obligation was for some time strenuously resisted by the natives of Amoy, Swatow, and elsewhere in that neighborhood. At length, when compelled to yield, it is said that they sullenly wound their queues round their heads and covered them with turbans, which are still worn by natives of those parts.

The peculiar custom of shaving the head in front, and allowing the hair to grow long behind, is said to have been adopted by the Manchus out of affectionate gratitude to the horse, an animal which has played an all-important part in the history and achievements of the race. This view is greatly reinforced by the cut of the modern official sleeves, which hang down, concealing the hands, and are shaped exactly like a pair of horse's hoofs.

In many respects the Manchu conquerors left the Chinese to follow their own customs. No attempt was made to coerce Chinese women, who dress their hair in styles totally different from that of the Manchu women; there are, too, some tolerated differences between the dress of the Manchu and Chinese men, but these are such as readily escape notice. Neither was any attempt made in the opening years of the conquest to interfere with foot-binding by Chinese women; but in 1664 an edict was issued forbidding the practice. Readers may draw their own conclusions, when it is added that four years after the edict was withdrawn. Hopes are now widely and earnestly entertained that with the dawn of the new era, this cruel custom will become a thing of the past; it is, however, to be feared that those who have been urging on this desirable reform may be, like all reformers, a little too sanguine of immediate success, and that a comparatively long period will have to go by before the last traces of foot-binding disappear altogether. Meanwhile, it seems that the Government has taken the important step of refusing admission to the public schools of all girls whose feet are bound.

The disappearance of the queue is another thing altogether. It is not a native Chinese institution; there would be no violation of any cherished tradition of antiquity if it were once and for ever discarded. On the contrary, if the Chinese do not intend to follow the Japanese and take to foreign clothes, there might be a return to the old style of doing the hair. The former dress of the Japanese was one of the numerous items borrowed by them from China; it was indeed the national dress of the Chinese for some three hundred years, between A.D. 600-900. One little difficulty will vanish with the queue. A Chinese coolie will tie his tail round his head when engaged on work in which he requires to keep it out of the way, and the habit has become of real importance with the use of modern machinery; but on the arrival of his master, he should at once drop it, out of respect, a piece of politeness not always exhibited in the presence of a foreign employer. The agitation, now in progress, for the final abolition of the queue may be due to one or all of the following reasons. Intelligent Chinese may have come to realize that the fashion is cumbrous and out of date. Sensitive Chinese may fear that it makes them ridiculous in the eyes of foreigners. Political Chinese, who would gladly see the re-establishment of a native dynasty, may look to its disappearance as the first step towards throwing off the Manchu yoke.

On the whole, the ruling Manchus have shown themselves very careful not to wound the susceptibilities of their Chinese subjects. Besides allowing the women to retain their own costume, and the dead, men and women alike, to be buried in the costume of the previous dynasty, it was agreed from the very first that no Chinese concubines should be taken into the Palace. This last condition seems to be a concession pure and simple to the conquered; there is little doubt, however, that the wily Manchus were only too ready to exclude a very dangerous possibility of political intrigue.

CHAPTER VI

LITERATURE AND EDUCATION

The Chinese people reverence above all things literature and learning; they hate war, bearing in mind the saying of Mencius, "There is no such thing as a *righteous* war; we can only assert that some wars are better than others;" and they love trade and the finesse of the market-place. China can boast many great soldiers, in modern as well as in ancient days; but anything like a proper appreciation of the military arm is of quite recent growth. "Good iron is not used for nails, nor good men for soldiers," says the proverb; and again, "One stroke of the civilian's pen reduces the military official to abject submission." On the other hand, it is admitted that "Civilians give the empire peace, and soldiers give it security."

Chinese parents have never, until recent days, willingly trained their sons for the army. They have always wished their boys to follow the stereotyped literary curriculum, and then, after passing successfully through the great competitive examinations, to rise to high civil office in the state. A good deal of ridicule has been heaped of late on the Chinese competitive examination, the subjects of which were drawn exclusively from the Confucian Canon, and included a knowledge of ancient history, of a comprehensive scheme of morality, initiated by Confucius, and further elaborated by Mencius (372-289 B.C.), of the ballads and ceremonial rites of three thousand years ago, and of an aptitude for essay-writing and the composition of verse. The whole curriculum may be fitly compared with such an education as was given to William Pitt and others among our own great statesmen, in which an ability to read the Greek and Roman classics, coupled with an intimate knowledge of the Peloponnesian War, carried the student about as far as it was considered necessary for him to go. The Chinese course, too, has certainly brought to the front in its time a great many eminent men, who have held their own in diplomacy, if not in warfare, with the subtlest intellects of the West.

Their system of competitive examinations has indeed served the Chinese well. It is the brightest spot in the whole administration, being absolutely above suspicion, such as attaches to other departments of the state. Attempts have been made from time to time to gain admission by improper means to the list of successful candidates, and it would be absurd to say that not one has ever succeeded; the risk, however, is too great, for the penalty on detection may be death.

The ordeal itself is exceedingly severe, as well for the examiners as for the candidates. At the provincial examinations, held once in every third year, an Imperial Commissioner, popularly known as the Grand Examiner, is sent down from Peking. On arrival, his residence is formally sealed up, and extraordinary precautions are taken to prevent friends of intending candidates from approaching him in any way. There is no age limit, and men of quite mature years are to be found competing against youths hardly out of their teens; indeed, there is an authenticated case of a man who successfully graduated at the age of seventy-two. Many compete year after year, until at length they decide to give it up as a bad job.

At an early hour on the appointed day the candidates begin to assemble, and by and by the great gates of the examination hall are thrown open, and heralds shriek out the names of those who are to enter. Each one answers in turn as his name is called, and receives from the attendants a roll of paper marked with the number of the open cell he is to occupy in one of the long alleys into which the examination hall is divided. Other writing materials, as well as food, he carries with him in a basket, which is always carefully searched at the door, and in which "sleeve" editions of the classics have sometimes been found. When all have taken their seats, the Grand Examiner burns incense, and closes the entrance gates, through which no one will be allowed to pass, either in or out, dead or alive, until the end of the third day, when the first of the three sessions is at an end, and the candidates are released for the night. In case of death, not unusual where ten or twelve thousand persons are cooped up day and night in a confined space, the corpse is hoisted over the wall; and this would be done even if it were that of the Grand Examiner himself, whose place would then be taken by the chief Assistant Examiner, who is also appointed by the Emperor, and accompanies the Grand Examiner from Peking.

The long strain of three bouts of three days each has often been found sufficient to unhinge the reason, with a variety of distressing consequences, the least perhaps of which may be seen in a regular percentage of blank papers handed in. On one occasion, a man handed in a copy of his last will and testament; on another, not very long ago, the mental balance of the Grand Examiner gave way, and a painful scene ensued. He tore up a number of the papers already handed in, and bit and kicked every one who came near him, until he was finally secured and bound hand and foot in his chair. A candidate once presented himself dressed in woman's clothes, with his face highly rouged and powdered, as is the custom. He was arrested at the entrance gate, and quietly sent home to his friends.

Overwork, in the feverish desire to get into the Government service, is certainly responsible for the mental break-down of a large proportion of the comparatively few lunatics found in China. There being no lunatic asylums

67

in the empire, it is difficult to form anything like an exact estimate of their number; it can only be said, what is equally true of cripples or deformed persons, that it is very rare to meet them in the streets or even to hear of their existence.

As a further measure of precaution against corrupt practices at examinations, the papers handed in by the candidates are all copied out in red ink, and only these copies are submitted to the examiners. The difficulty therefore of obtaining favorable treatment, on the score of either bribery or friendship, is very much increased. The Chinese, who make no attempt to conceal or excuse, in fact rather exaggerate any corruption in their public service generally, do not hesitate to declare with striking unanimity that the conduct of their examination system is above suspicion, and there appears to be no valid reason why we should not accept this conclusion.

The whole system is now undergoing certain modifications, which, if wisely introduced, should serve only to strengthen the national character. The Confucian teachings, which are of the very highest order of morality, and which have molded the Chinese people for so many centuries, helping perhaps to give them a cohesion and stability remarkable among the nations of the world, should not be lightly cast aside. A scientific training, enabling us to annihilate time and space, to extend indefinitely the uses and advantages of matter in all its forms, and to mitigate the burden of suffering which is laid upon the greater portion of the human race, still requires to be effectively supplemented by a moral training, to teach man his duty towards his neighbor. From the point of view of science, the Chinese are, of course, wholly out of date, though it is only within the past hundred and fifty years that the West has so decisively outstripped the East. If we go back to the fifteenth century, we shall find that the standard of civilization, as the term is usually understood, was still much higher in China than in Europe; while Marco Polo, the famous Venetian traveler of the thirteenth century, who actually lived twenty-four years in China, and served as an official under Kublai Khan, has left it on record that the magnificence of Chinese cities, and the splendor of the Chinese court, outrivaled anything he had ever seen or heard of.

Pushing farther back into antiquity, we easily reach a time when the inhabitants of the Middle Kingdom "held learning in high esteem, while our own painted forefathers were running naked and houseless in the woods, and living on berries and raw meat." In inventive, mechanical and engineering aptitudes the Chinese have always excelled; as witness—only to mention a few—the art of printing (*see below*); their water-wheels and other clever appliances for irrigation; their wonderful bridges (not to mention the Great Wall); the "taxicab," or carriage fitted with a machine for recording the distance traversed, the earliest notice of which takes us back to the fourth century A.D.; the system of fingerprints for personal identification, recorded in the seventh century A.D.; the carved ivory balls which contain even so many as nine or ten other balls, of diminishing size, one within another; a chariot carrying a figure which always pointed south, recorded as in existence at a very early date, though unfortunately the specifications which have came down to us from later dates will not work out, as in the case of the "taxicab." The story goes that this chariot was invented about 1100 B.C., by a wonderful hero of the day, in order to enable an ambassador, who had come to the court of China from a far distant country in the south, to find his way expeditiously home. The compass proper the Chinese cannot claim; it was probably introduced into China by the Arabs at a comparatively late date, and has been confused with the south-pointing chariot of earlier ages. As to gunpowder, something of that nature appears to have been used for fireworks in the seventh century; and something of the nature of a gun is first heard of during the Mongol campaigns of the thirteenth century; but firearms were not systematically employed until the fifteenth century. Add to the above the art of casting bronze, brought to a high pitch of excellence seven or eight centuries before the Christian era, if not earlier; the production of silk, mentioned by Mencius (372-289 B.C.) as necessary for the comfort of old age; the cultivation of the tea-plant from time immemorial; also the discovery and manufacture of porcelain some sixteen centuries ago, subsequently brought to a perfection which leaves all European attempts hopelessly out-classed.

In many instances the Chinese seem to have been so near and yet so far. There is a distinct tradition of flying cars at a very remote date; and rough woodcuts have been handed down for many centuries, showing a car containing two passengers, flying through the clouds and apparently propelled by wheels of a screw pattern, set at right angles to the direction in which the travelers are proceeding. But there is not a scrap of evidence to show what was the motive power which turned the wheels. Similarly, iron ships are mentioned in Chinese literature so far back as the tenth century, only, however, to be ridiculed as an impossibility; the circulation of the blood is hinted at; added to which is the marvelous anticipation of anaesthetics as applied to surgery, to be mentioned later on, an idea which also remained barren of results for something like sixteen centuries, until Western science stepped in and secured the prize. Here it may be fairly argued that, considering the national repugnance to mutilation of the body in any form, it could hardly be expected that the Chinese would seek to facilitate a process to which they so strongly object.

In the domain of painting, we are only just beginning to awake to the fact that in this direction the Chinese have reached heights denied to all save artists of supreme power, and that their art was already on a lofty level many centuries before our own great representatives had begun to put brush to canvas. Without going so far back as the famous picture in the British Museum, by an artist of the fourth and fifth centuries A.D., the point may perhaps be

70

emphasized by quotation from the words of a leading art-critic, referring to painters of the tenth and eleventh centuries:—"To the Sung artists and poets, mountains were a passion, as to Wordsworth. The landscape art thus founded, and continued by the Japanese in the fifteenth century, must rank as the greatest school of landscape which the world has seen. It is the imaginative picturing of what is most elemental and most august in Nature—liberating visions of storm or peace among abrupt peaks, plunging torrents, trembling reed-beds—and though having a fantastic side for its weakness, can never have the reproach of pretty tameness and mere fidelity which form too often the only ideal of Western landscape."

Great Chinese artists unite in dismissing fidelity to outline as of little importance compared with reproduction of the spirit of the object painted. To paint a tree successfully, it is necessary to produce not merely shape and color but the vitality and "soul" of the original. Until with the last two or three centuries, nature itself was always appealed to as the one source of true inspiration; then came the artist of the studio, since which time Chinese art has languished, while Japanese art, learned at the feet of Chinese artists from the fourteenth century onwards, has come into prominent notice, and is now, with extraordinary versatility, attempting to assimilate the ideals of the West.

The following words were written by a Chinese painter of the fifth century:—

"To gaze upon the clouds of autumn, a soaring exaltation in the soul; to feel the spring breeze stirring wild exultant thoughts;—what is there in the possession of gold and gems to compare with delights like these? And then, to unroll the portfolio and spread the silk, and to transfer to it the glories of flood and fell, the green forest, the blowing winds, the white water of the rushing cascade, as with a turn of the hand a divine influence descends upon the scene. . . . These are the joys of painting."

Just as in poetry, so in pictorial art, the artist avoids giving full expression to his theme, and leaving nothing for the spectator to supply by his own imaginative powers. "Suggestion" is the key-note to both the above arts; and in both, "Impressionism" has been also at the command of the gifted, centuries before the term had passed into the English language.

Literature and art are indeed very closely associated in China. Every literary man is supposed to be more or less a painter, or a musician of sorts; failing personal skill, it would go without saying that he was a critic, or at the lowest a lover, of one or the other art, or of both. All Chinese men, women and children seem to love flowers; and the poetry which has gathered around the blossoms of plum and almond alone would form a not inconsiderable library of itself. Yet a European bouquet would appear to a man of culture as little short of a monstrosity; for to enjoy flowers, a Chinaman must see only a single spray at a time. The poorly paid clerk will bring with him to his office in the morning some trifling bud, which he will stick into a tiny vase of water, and place beside him on his desk. The owner of what may be a whole gallery of pictures will invite you to tea, followed by an inspection of his treasures; but on the same afternoon he will only produce perhaps a single specimen, and scout the idea that any one could call for more. If a long landscape, it will be gradually unwound from its roller, and a portion at a time will be submitted for the enjoyment and criticism of his visitors; if a religious or historical picture, or a picture of birds or flowers, of which the whole effort must be viewed in its completeness, it will be studied in various senses, during the intervals between a chat and a cup of tea. Such concentration is absolutely essential, in the eyes of the Chinese critic, to a true interpretation of the artist's meaning, and to a just appreciation of his success.

The marvelous old stories of grapes painted by Zeuxis of ancient Greece, so naturally that birds came to peck at them; and of the curtain painted by Parrhasius which Zeuxis himself tried to pull aside; and of the horse by Apelles at which another horse neighed—all these find their counterparts in the literature of Chinese art. One painter, in quite early days, painted a perch and hung it over a river bank, when there was immediately a rush of otters to secure it. Another painted the creases on cotton clothes so exactly that the clothes looked as if they had just come from the wash. Another produced pictures of cats which would keep a place free from rats. All these efforts were capped by those of another artist, whose picture of the North Wind made people feel cold, while his picture of the South Wind made people feel hot. Such exaggerations are not altogether without their value; they suggest that Chinese art must have reached a high level, and this has recently been shown to be nothing more than the truth, by the splendid exhibition of Chinese pictures recently on view in the British Museum.

The literary activities of the Chinese, and their output of literature, have always been on a colossal scale; and of course it is entirely due to the early invention of printing that, although a very large number of works have disappeared, still an enormous bulk has survived the ravages of war, rebellion and fire.

This art was rather developed than invented. There is no date, within a margin even of half a century either way, at which we can say that printing was invented. The germ is perhaps to be found in the engraving of seals, which have been used by the Chinese as far back as we can go with anything like historical certainty, and also of stone tablets from which rubbings were taken, the most important of these being the forty-six tablets on which five of the sacred books of Confucianism were engraved about A.D. 170, and of which portions still remain. However this may be, it was during the sixth century A.D. that the idea of taking impressions on paper from wooden blocks seems to have arisen, chiefly in connection with religious pictures and tracts. It was not widely applied to the production of books in general until A.D. 932, when the Confucian Canon was so printed for the first time; from which point onwards the extension of the art moved with rapid strides.

It is very noticeable that the Chinese, who are extraordinarily averse to novelties, and can hardly be induced to consider any innovations, when once convinced of their real utility, waste no further time in securing to themselves all the advantages which may accrue. This was forcibly illustrated in regard to the introduction of the telegraph, against which the Chinese had set their faces, partly because of the disturbance of geomantic influences caused by the tall telegraph poles, and partly because they sincerely doubted that the wires could achieve the results claimed. But when it was discovered that some wily Cantonese had learnt over the telegraph the names of the three highest graduates at the Peking triennial examination, weeks before the names could be known in Canton by the usual route, and had enriched himself by buying up the tickets bearing those names in the great lotteries which are always held in connection with this event, Chinese opposition went down like a house of cards; and the only question with many of the literati was whether, at some remote date, the Chinese had not invented telegraphy themselves.

Moveable types of baked clay were invented about A.D. 1043, and some centuries later they were made of wood and of copper or lead; but they have never gained the favor accorded to block-printing, by which most of the great literary works have been produced. The newspapers of modern days are all printed from moveable types, and also many translations of foreign books, prepared to meet the increasing demand for Western learning. The Chinese have always been a great reading people, systematic education culminating in competitive examinations for students going back to the second century A.D. This is perhaps a suitable place for explaining that the famous *Peking Gazette*, often said to be the oldest newspaper in the world, is not really a newspaper at all, in that it contains no news in our sense of the term. It is a record only of court movements, list of promoted officials, with a few selected memorials and edicts. It is published daily, but was not printed until the fifteenth century.

Every Chinese boy may be said to have his chance. The slightest sign of a capacity for book-learning is watched for, even among the poorest. Besides the opportunity of free schools, a clever boy will soon find a patron; and in many cases, the funds for carrying on a curriculum, and for entering the first of the great competitions, will be subscribed in the district, on which the candidate will confer a lasting honor by his success. A promising young graduate, who has won his first degree with honors, is at once an object of importance to wealthy fathers who desire to secure him as a son-in-law, and who will see that money is not wanting to carry him triumphantly up the official ladder. Boys without any gifts of the kind required, remain to fill the humbler positions; those who advance to a certain point are drafted into trade; while hosts of others who just fall short of the highest, become tutors in private families, schoolmasters, doctors, fortune-tellers, geomancers, and booksellers' hacks.

Of high-class Chinese literature, it is not possible to give even the faintest idea in the space at disposal. It must suffice to say that all branches are adequately represented, histories, biographies, philosophy, poetry and essays on all manner of subjects, offering a wide field even to the most insatiate reader.

And here a remark may be interjected, which is very necessary for the information of those who wish to form a true estimate of the Chinese people. Throughout the Confucian Canon, a collection of ancient works on which the moral code of the Chinese is based, there is not a single word which could give offence, even to the most sensitive, on questions of delicacy and decency. That is surely saying a good deal, but it is not all; precisely the same may be affirmed of what is mentioned above as high-class Chinese literature, which is pure enough to satisfy the most strait-laced. Chinese poetry, of which there is in existence a huge mass, will be searched in vain for suggestions of impropriety, for sly innuendo, and for the other tricks of the unclean. This extraordinary purity of language is all the more remarkable from the fact that, until recent years, the education of women has not been at all general, though many particular instances are recorded of women who have themselves achieved success in literary pursuits. It is only when we come to the novel, to the short story, or to the anecdote, which are not usually written in high-class style, and are therefore not recognized as literature proper, that this exalted standard is no longer always maintained.

There are, indeed, a great number of novels, chiefly historical and religious, in which the aims of the writers are on a sufficiently high level to keep them clear of what is popularly known as pornography or pig-writing; still, when all is said and done, there remains a balance of writing curiously in contrast with the great bulk of Chinese literature proper. As to the novel, the long story with a worked-out plot, this is not really a local product. It seems to have come along with the Mongols from Central Asia, when they conquered China in the thirteenth century, and established their short-lived dynasty. Some novels, in spite of their low moral tone, are exceedingly well written and clever, graphic in description, and dramatic in episode; but it is curious that no writer of the first rank has ever attached his name to a novel, and that the authorship of all the cleverest is a matter of entire uncertainty.

The low-class novel is purposely pitched in a style that will be easily understood; but even so, there is a great deal of word- and phrase-skipping to be done by many illiterate readers, who are quite satisfied if they can extract the general sense as they go along. The book-language, as cultivated by the best writers, is to be freely understood only by those who have stocked their minds well with the extensive phraseology which has been gradually created by eminent men during the past twenty-five centuries, and with historical and biographical allusions and references of all sorts and things. A word or two, suggesting some apposite allusion, will often greatly enhance the beauty of a composition for the connoisseur, but will fall flat on the ears of those to whom the quotation is unknown. Simple objects in everyday life often receive quaint names, as handed down in literature, with which it is necessary to be familiar. For instance, a "fairy umbrella" means a mushroom; a "gentleman of the beam" is a burglar, because a burglar was once caught sitting on one of the open beams inside a Chinese roof; a "slender waist" is a wasp; the "throat olive" is the "Adam's apple"—which, by the way, is an excellent illustration from the opposite point of view; "eyebrow notes" means notes at the top of a page; "cap words" is sometimes used for "preface;" the "sweeper-away of care" is wine; "golden balls" are oranges; the "golden tray" is the moon; a "two-haired man" is a grey-beard; the "hundred holes" is a beehive; "instead of the moon" is a lantern; "instead of steps" is a horse; "the man with the wooden skirt" is a shopman; to "scatter sleep" means to give hush-money; and so on, almost *ad infinitum.*

Chinese medical literature is on a very voluminous scale, medicine having always occupied a high place in the estimation of the people, in spite of the fact that its practice has always been left to any one who might choose to take it up. Surgery, even of an elementary kind, has never had a chance; for the Chinese are extremely loath to suffer any interference with their bodies, believing, in accordance with Confucian dogma, that as they received them from their parents, so they should carry them into the presence of their ancestors in the next world. Medicine, as still practiced in China, may be compared with the European art of a couple of centuries ago, and its exceedingly doubtful results are fully appreciated by patients at large. "No medicine," says one proverb, "is better than a middling doctor;" while another points out that "Many sons of clever doctors die of disease."

Legend, however, tells us of an extraordinary physician of the fifth century B.C. who was able to see into the viscera of his patients—an apparent anticipation of the X-rays—and who, by his intimate knowledge of the human pulse, effected many astounding cures. We also read of an eminent physician of the second and third centuries A.D. who did add surgery to this other qualifications. He was skilled in the use of acupuncture and cautery; but if these failed he would render his patient unconscious by a dose of hashish, and then operate surgically. He is said to have diagnosed a case of diseased bowels by the pulse alone, and then to have cured it by operation. He offered to cure the headaches of a famous military commander of the day by opening his skull under hashish; but the offer was rudely declined. This story serves to show, in spite of its marvelous setting, that the idea of administering an anaesthetic to carry out a surgical operation must be credited, so far as priority goes, to the Chinese, since the book in which the above account is given cannot have been composed later than the twelfth century A.D.

CHAPTER VII

PHILOSOPHY AND SPORT

Chinese philosophy covers altogether too large a field to be dealt with, even in outline, on a scale suitable to this volume; only a few of its chief features can possibly be exhibited in the space at disposal.

Beginning with moral philosophy, we are confronted at once with what was in early days an extremely vexed question; not perhaps entirely set at rest even now, but allowed to remain in suspense amid the universal acceptance of Confucian teachings. Confucius himself taught in no indistinct terms that man is born good, and that he becomes evil only by contact with evil surroundings. He does not enlarge upon this dogma, but states it baldly as a natural law, little anticipating that within a couple of centuries it was to be called seriously in question. It remained for his great follower, Mencius, born a hundred years later, to defend the proposition against all comers, and especially against one of no mean standing, the philosopher Kao (*Cow*). Kao declared that righteousness is only to be got out of man's nature in the same way that good cups and bowls are to be got out of a block of willow wood, namely, by care in fashioning them. Improper workmanship would produce bad results; good workmanship, on the other hand, would produce good results. In plain words, the nature of man at birth is neither good nor bad; and what it becomes afterwards depends entirely upon what influences have been brought to bear and in what surroundings it has come to maturity.

Mencius met this argument by showing that in the process of extracting cups and bowls from a block of wood, the wood as a block is destroyed, and he pointed out that, according to such reasoning, man's nature would also be destroyed in the process of getting righteousness out of it.

Again, Kao maintained that man's nature has as little concern with good or evil as water has with east or west; for water will flow indifferently either one way or the other, according to the conditions in each case. If there is freedom on the east, it will flow east; if there is freedom on the west, it will flow west; and so with human nature, which will move similarly in the direction of either good or evil. In reply, Mencius freely admitted that water would flow either east or west; but he asked if it would flow indifferently up or down. He then declared that the bent of human nature towards good is precisely like the tendency of water to flow down and not up. You can force water to jump up, he said, by striking it, and by mechanical appliances you can make it flow to the top of a hill; but what you do in such cases is entirely contrary to the nature of water, and is merely the result of violence, such violence, in fact, as is brought into play when man's nature is bent towards evil.

"That which men get at birth," said Kao, "is their nature," implying that all natures were the same, just as the whiteness of a white feather is the same as the whiteness of white snow; whereupon Mencius showed that on this principle the nature of a dog would be the same as that of a an ox, or the nature of an ox the same as that of a man. Finally, Mencius declared that for whatever evil men may commit, their natures can in nowise be blamed. In prosperous times, he argued, men are mostly good, whereas in times of scarcity the opposite is the case; these two conditions, however, are not to be charged against the natures with which God sent them into the world, but against the circumstances in which the individuals in question have been situated.

The question, however, of man's original nature was not set permanently at rest by the arguments of Mencius. A philosopher, named Hsun Tzu (*Sheundza*), who flourished not very much later than Mencius, came forward with the theory that so far from being good according to Confucius, or even neutral according to Kao, the nature of man at birth is positively evil. He supports this view by the following arguments. From his earliest years, man is actuated by a love of gain for his own personal enjoyment. His conduct is distinguished by selfishness and combativeness. He becomes a slave to envy, hatred, and other passions. The restraint of law, and the influence and guidance of teachers, are absolutely necessary to good government and the well-being of social life. Just as wood must be subjected to pressure in order to make it straight, and metal must be subjected to the grindstone in order to make it sharp, so must the nature of man be subjected to training and education in order to obtain from it the virtues of justice and self-sacrifice which characterize the best of the human race. It is impossible to maintain that man's nature is good in the same sense that his eyes see and his ears hear; for in the latter there is no alternative. An eye which does not see, is not an eye; an ear which does not hear, is not an ear. This proves that whereas seeing and hearing are natural to man, goodness is artificial and acquired. Just as a potter produces a dish or a carpenter a bench, working on some material before them, so do the sages and teachers of mankind produce righteousness by working upon the nature of man, which they transform in the same way that the potter transforms the clay or the carpenter the wood. We cannot believe that God has favorites, and deals unkindly with others. How, then, is it that some men are evil while others are good? The answer is, that the former follow their natural disposition, while the latter submit to restraints and follow the guidance of their teachers. It is indeed true that any one may become a hero, but all men do not necessarily become heroes, nor is there any method by which they can be forced to do so. If a man is endowed with a capacity for improvement, and is placed in the hands of good teachers, associating at the same time with friends whose actions display such virtues as self-sacrifice, truth, kindness, and so forth, he will naturally imbibe principles which will raise him to the same standard; whereas, if he consorts with evil livers, he will be a daily witness of deceit, corruption, and general impurity of conduct, and will gradually lapse into the same course of life. If you do not know your son, says the proverb, look at his friends.

The next step was taken by the philosopher Yang Hsiung (*Sheeyoong*), 53 B.C. to A.D. 18. He started a theory which occupies a middle place between the last two theories discussed above, teaching that the nature of man at birth is neither wholly good nor wholly evil, but a mixture of both, and that development in either direction depends altogether on environment. A compromise in matters of faith is not nearly so picturesque as an extreme, and Yang's attempted solution has attracted but scant attention, though always mentioned with respect. The same may also be said of another attempt to smooth obvious difficulties in the way of accepting either of the two extremes or the middle course proposed by Yang Hsiung. The famous Han Yu, to be mentioned again shortly, was a pillar and prop of Confucianism. He flourished between A.D. 768 and 824, and performed such lasting services in what was to him the cause of truth, that his tablet has been placed in the Confucian temple, an honor reserved only for those whose orthodoxy is beyond suspicion. Yet he ventured upon an attempt to modify this important dogma, taking care all the time to appear as if he were criticizing Mencius rather than Confucius, on whom, of course, the real responsibility rests. He declared, solely upon his own authority, that the nature of man is not uniform but divided into three grades—namely, highest, middle, and lowest. Thus, natures of the highest grade are good, wholly good, and nothing but good; natures of the lowest grade are evil, wholly evil, and nothing but evil; while natures of the middle grade may, under right direction, rise to the highest grade, or, under wrong direction, sink to the lowest.

Another question, much debated in the age of Mencius, arose out of the rival statements of two almost contemporary philosophers, Mo Ti (*Maw Tee*) and Yang Chu. The former taught a system of mutual and consequently universal love as a cure for all the ills arising from misgovernment and want of social harmony. He pointed out, with much truth, that if the feudal states would leave one another alone, families cease to quarrel, and thieves cease to steal, while sovereign and subject lived on terms of benevolence and loyalty, and fathers and sons on terms of kindness and filial piety—then indeed the empire would be well governed. But beyond suggesting the influence of teachers in the prohibition of hatred and the encouragement of mutual love, our philosopher does little or nothing to aid us in reaching such a desirable consummation.

The doctrine of Yang Chu is summed up as "every man for himself," and is therefore diametrically opposed to that of Mo Ti. A questioner one day asked him if he would consent to part with a single hair in order to benefit the whole world. Yang Chu replied that a single hair could be of no possible benefit to the world; and on being further pressed to say what he would do if a hair were really of such benefit, it is stated that he gave no answer. On the strength of this story, Mencius said: "Yang's principle was, every man for himself. Though by plucking out a single hair he might have benefited the whole world, he would not have done so. Mo's system was universal love. If by taking off every hair from the crown of his head to the sole of his foot he could have benefited the empire, he would have done so. Neither of these two doctrines is sound; a middle course is the right one."

The origin of the visible universe is a question on which Chinese philosophers have very naturally been led to speculate. Legend provides us with a weird being named

P'an Ku, who came into existence, no one can quite say how, endowed with perfect knowledge, his function being to set the gradually developing universe in order. He is often represented pictorially with a huge adze in his hand, and engaged in constructing the world out of the matter which has just begun to take shape. With his death the detailed part of creation appeared. His breath became the wind; his voice, the thunder; his left eye, the sun; his right eye, the moon; his blood yielded rivers; his hair grew into trees and plants; his flesh became the soil; his sweat descended as rain; and the parasites which infested his body were the forerunners of the human race. This sort of stuff, however, could only appeal to the illiterate; for intellectual and educated persons something more was required. And so it came about that a system, based originally upon the quite incomprehensible Book of Changes, generally regarded as the oldest portion of the Confucian Canon, was gradually elaborated and brought to a finite state during the eleventh and twelfth centuries of our era. According to this system, there was a time, almost beyond the reach of expression in figures, when nothing at all existed. In the period which followed, there came into existence, spontaneously, a principle, which after another lapse of time resolved itself into two principles with entirely opposite characteristics. One of these principles represented light, heat, masculinity, and similar phenomena classed as positive; the other represented darkness, cold, femininity, and other phenomena classed as negative. The interaction of these two principles in duly adjusted proportions produced the five elements, earth, fire, water, wood, and metal; and with their assistance all Nature as we see it around us was easily and rapidly developed. Such is the Confucian theory, at any rate so called, for it cannot be shown that Confucius ever entertained these notions, and his alleged connection with the Canon of Changes is itself of doubtful authenticity.

Chuang Tzu (*Chwongdza*), a philosopher of the third and fourth centuries B.C., who was not only a mystic but also a moralist and a social reformer, has something to say on the subject: "If there is existence, there must have been non-existence. And if there was a time when nothing existed, then there must have been a time before that, when even nothing did not exist. Then when nothing came into existence, could one really say whether it belonged to existence or non-existence?"

"Nothing" was rather a favorite term with Chuang Tzu for the exercise of his wit. Light asked Nothing, saying: "Do you, sir, exist, or do you not exist?" But getting no answer to his question, Light set to work to watch for the appearance of Nothing. Hidden, vacuous—all day long he looked but could not see it, listened but could not hear it, grasped at but could not seize it. "Bravo!" cried Light; "who can equal this? I can get to be nothing [meaning darkness], but I can't get to be not nothing."

Confucius would have nothing to say on the subject of death and a future state; his theme was consistently this life and its obligations, and he regarded speculation on the unknown as sheer waste of time. When one of three friends died and Confucius sent a disciple to condole with the other two, the disciple found them sitting by the side of the corpse, merrily singing and playing on the lute. They professed the then comparatively new faith which taught that life was a dream and death the awakening. They believed that at death the pure man "mounts to heaven, and roaming through the clouds, passes beyond the limits of space, oblivious of existence, for ever and ever without end." When the shocked disciple reported what he had seen, Confucius said, "These men travel beyond the rule of life; I travel within it. Consequently, our paths do not meet; and I was wrong in sending you to mourn. They look on life as a huge tumor from which death sets them free. All the same they know not where they were before birth, nor where they will be after death. They ignore their passions. They take no account of their ears and eyes. Backwards and forwards through all eternity, they do not admit a beginning or an end. They stroll beyond the dust and dirt of mortality, to wander in the realms of inaction. How should such men trouble themselves with the conventionalities of this world, or care what people may think of them?"

Life comes, says Chuang Tzu, and cannot be declined; it goes, and cannot be stopped. But alas, the world thinks that to nourish the physical frame is enough to preserve life. Although not enough, it must still be done; this cannot be neglected. For if one is to neglect the physical frame, better far to retire at once from the world, since by renouncing the world one gets rid of the cares of the world. There is, however, the vitality which informs the physical frame; that must be equally an object of incessant care. Then he whose physical frame is perfect and whose vitality remains in its original purity—he is one with God. Man passes through this sublunary life as a sunbeam passes through a crack; here one moment, and gone the next. Neither are there any not equally subject to the ingress and egress of mortality. One modification brings life; then comes another, and there is death. Living creatures cry out; human beings feel sorrow. The bow-case is slipped off; the clothes'-bag is dropped; and in the confusion the soul wings its flight, and the body follows, on the great journey home.

Attention has already been drawn to this necessary cultivation of the physical frame, and Chuan Tzu gives an instance of the extent to which it was carried. There was a certain man whose nose was covered with a very hard scab, which was at the same time no thicker than a fly's wing. He sent for a stonemason to chip it off; and the latter plied his adze with great dexterity while the patient sat absolutely rigid, without moving a muscle, and let him chip. When the scab was all off, the nose was found to be quite uninjured. Such skill was of course soon noised abroad, and a feudal prince, who also had a scab on his nose, sent for the mason to take it off. The mason, however, declined to try, alleging that the success did not depend so much upon the skill of the operator as upon the mental control of the patient by which the physical frame became as it were a perfectly inanimate object.

Contemporary with Chuang Tzu, but of a very different school of thought, was the philosopher Hui Tzu (*Hooeydza*). He was particularly fond of the quibbles which so delighted the sophists or unsound reasoners of ancient Greece. Chuang Tzu admits that he was a man of many ideas, and that his works would fill five carts—this, it must be remembered, because they were written on slips of wood tied together by a string run through eyelets. But he adds that Hui Tzu's doctrines are paradoxical, and his terms used ambiguously. Hui Tzu argued, for instance, that such abstractions as hardness and whiteness were separate existences, of which the mind could only be conscious separately, one at a time. He declared that there are feathers in a new-laid egg, because they ultimately appear on the chick. He maintained that fire is not hot; it is the man who feels hot. That the eye does not see; it is the man who sees. That compasses will not make a circle; it is the man. That a bay horse and a dun cow are three; because taken separately they are two, and taken together they are one: two and one make three. That a motherless colt never had a mother; when it had a mother, it was not motherless. That if you take a stick a foot long and every day cut it in half, you will never come to the end of it.

Of what use, asked his great rival, is Hui Tzu to the world? His efforts can only be compared with those of a gadfly or a mosquito. He makes a noise to drown an echo. He is like a man running a race with his own shadow.

When Chuang Tzu was about to die, his disciples expressed a wish to give him a splendid funeral. But Chuang Tzu said: "With heaven and earth for my coffin and my shell; with the sun, moon and stars as my burial regalia; and with all creation to escort me to my grave,— are not my funeral paraphernalia ready to hand?" "We fear," argued the disciples, "lest the carrion kite should eat the body of our Master;" to which Chuang Tzu replied:

"Above ground I shall be food for kites; below ground for mole-crickets and ants. Why rob one to feed the other?"

Life in China is not wholly made up of book-learning and commerce. The earliest Chinese records exhibit the people as following the chase in the wake of the great nobles, more as a sport than as the serious business it must have been in still more remote ages; and the first emperors of the present dynasty were also notable sportsmen, who organized periodical hunting-tours on a scale of considerable magnificence.

Hawking was practiced at least so far back as a century before Christ; for we have a note on a man of that period who "loved to gallop after wily animals with horse and dog, or follow up with falcon the pheasant and the hare." The sport may be seen in northern China at the present day. A hare is put up, and a couple of native greyhounds are dispatched after it; these animals, however, would soon be distanced by the hare, which can run straight away from them without doubling, but for the sudden descent of the falcon, and a blow from its claw, often stunning the hare at the first attempt, and enabling the dogs to come up.

Sportsmen who have to make their living by the business frequently descend to methods which are sometimes very ingenious, and more remunerative than the gun, but can hardly be classified as sport. Thus, a man in search of wild duck will mark down a flock settled on some shallow sheet of water. He will then put a crate over his head and shoulders, and gradually approach the flock as though the crate were drifting on the surface. Once among them, he puts out a hand under water, seizes hold of a duck's legs, and rapidly pulls the bird down. The sudden disappearance of a colleague does not seem to trouble its companions, and in a short time a very considerable bag has been obtained. Tradition says that Confucius was fond of sport, but would never let fly at birds sitting; which, considering that his weapon was a bow-and-arrow, must be set down as a marvel of self-restraint.

Scores of Chinese poets have dwelt upon the joys of angling, and fishing is widely carried on over the inland waters; but the rod, except as a matter of pure sport, has given place to the businesslike net. The account of the use of fishing cormorants was formerly regarded as a traveler's tale. It is quite true, however, that small rafts carrying several of these birds, with a fisherman gently sculling at the stern, may be seen on the rivers of southern China. The cormorant seizes a passing fish, and the fisherman takes the fish from its beak. The bird is trained with a ring round its neck, which prevents it from swallowing the prey; while for each capture it is rewarded with a small piece of fish. Well-trained cormorants can be trusted to fish without the restraint of the ring. Confucius, again, is said to have been fond of fishing, but he would not use a net; and there was another sage of antiquity who would not even use a hook, but fished with a straight piece of iron, apparently thinking that the advantage would be an unfair one as against the resources of the fish; and declaring openly that he would only take such fish as wished to be caught. By such simple narratives do the Chinese strive to convey great truths to childish ears.

Many sports were once common in China which have long since passed out of the national life, and exist only in the record of books. Among these may be mentioned "butting," a very ancient pastime, mentioned in history two centuries before the Christian era. The sport consisted in putting an ox-skin, horns and all, over the head, and then trying to knock one's adversary out of time by butting at him after the fashion of bulls, the result being, as the history of a thousand years later tells us, "smashed heads, broken arms, and blood running in the Palace yard."

The art of boxing, which included wrestling, had been practiced by the Chinese several centuries before butting was introduced. Its most accomplished exponents were subsequently found among the priests of a Buddhist monastery, built about A.D. 500; and it was undoubtedly from their successors that the Japanese acquired a knowledge of the modern *jiu-jitsu*, which is simply the equivalent of the old Chinese term meaning "gentle art." A few words from a chapter on "boxing" in a military work of the sixteenth century will give some idea of the scope of the Chinese sport.

"The body must be quick to move, the hands quick to take advantage, and the legs lightly planted but firm, so as to advance or retire with effect. In the flying leap of the leg lies the skill of the art; in turning the adversary upside down lies its ferocity; in planting a straight blow with the fist lies its rapidity; and in deftly holding the adversary face upwards lies its gentleness."

Football was played in China at a very early date; originally, with a ball stuffed full of hair; from the fifth century A.D., with an inflated bladder covered with leather. A picture of the goal, which is something like a triumphal arch, has come down to us, and also the technical names and positions of the players; even more than seventy kinds of kicks are enumerated, but the actual rules of the game are not known. It is recorded by one writer that "the winners were rewarded with flowers, fruit and wine, and even with silver bowls and brocades, while the captain of the losing team was flogged, and suffered other indignities." The game, which had disappeared for some centuries, is now being revived in Chinese schools and colleges under the control of foreigners, and finds great favour with the rising generation.

Polo is first mentioned in Chinese literature under the year A.D. 710, the reference being to a game played before the Emperor and his court. The game was very much in vogue for a long period, and even women were taught to play—on donkey-back. The Kitan Tartars were the most skilful players; it is doubtful if the game originated with them, or if it was introduced from Persia, with which country China had relations at a very early date. A statesman of the tenth century, disgusted at the way in which the Emperor played polo to excess, presented a long memorial, urging his Majesty to discontinue the practice. The reasons given for this advice were three in number. "(1) When sovereign and subject play together, there must be contention. If the sovereign wins, the subject is ashamed; if the former loses, the latter exults. (2) To jump on a horse and swing a mallet, galloping here and there, with no distinctions of rank, but only eager to be first and win, is destructive of all ceremony between sovereign and subject. (3) To make light of the responsibilities of empire, and run even the remotest risk of an accident, is to disregard obligations to the state and to her Imperial Majesty the Empress."

It has always been recognized that the chief duty of a statesman is to advise his master without fear or favor, and to protest loudly and openly against any course which is likely to be disadvantageous to the commonwealth, or to bring discredit on the court. It has also been always understood that such protests are made entirely at the risk of the statesman in question, who must be prepared to pay with his head for counsels which may be stigmatized as unpatriotic, though in reality they may be nothing more than unpalatable at the moment.

In the year A.D. 814 the Emperor, who had become a devout Buddhist, made arrangements for receiving with extravagant honors a bone of Buddha, which had been forwarded from India to be preserved as a relic. This was too much for Han Yu (already mentioned), the leading statesman of the day, who was a man of the people, raised by his own genius, and who, to make things worse, had already been banished eleven years previously for presenting an offensive Memorial on the subject of tax-collection, for which he had been forgiven and recalled. He promptly sent in a respectful but bitter denunciation of Buddha and all his works, and entreated his Majesty not to stain the Confucian purity of thought by tolerating such a degrading exhibition as that proposed. But for the intercession of friends, the answer to this bold memorial

91

would have been death; as it was he was banished to the neighborhood of the modern Swatow, then a wild and barbarous region, hardly incorporated into the Empire. There he set himself to civilize the rude inhabitants, until soon recalled and once more reinstated in office; and to this day there is a shrine dedicated to his memory, containing the following inscription: "Wherever he passed, he purified."

Another great statesman, who flourished over two hundred years later, and also several times suffered banishment, in an inscription to the honor and glory of his predecessor, put down the following words: "Truth began to be obscured and literature to fade; supernatural religions sprang up on all sides, and many eminent scholars failed to oppose their advance, until Han Yu, the cotton-clothed, arose and blasted them with his derisive sneer."

Since the fourteenth century there has existed a definite organization, known as the Censorate, the members of which, who are called the "ears and eyes" of the sovereign, make it their business to report adversely upon any course adopted by the Government in the name of the Emperor, or by any individual statesman, which seems to call for disapproval. The reproving Censor is nominally entitled to complete immunity from punishment; but in practice he knows that he cannot count too much upon either justice or mercy. If he concludes that his words will be unforgivable, he hands in his memorial, and draws public attention forthwith by committing suicide on the spot.

To be allowed to commit suicide, and not to suffer the indignity of a public execution, is a privilege sometimes extended to a high official whose life has become forfeit under circumstances which do not call for special degradation. A silken cord is forwarded from the Emperor to the official in question, who at once puts an end to his life, though not necessarily by strangulation. He may take poison, as is usually the case, and this is called "swallowing gold." For a long time it was believed that Chinese high officials really did swallow gold, which in view of its non-poisonous character gave rise to an idea that gold-leaf was employed, the leaf being inhaled and so causing suffocation. Some simple folk, Chinese as well as foreigners, believe this now, although native authorities have pointed out that workmen employed in the extraction of gold often steal pieces and swallow them, without any serious consequences whatever. Another explanation, which has also the advantage of being the true one, is that "swallowing gold" is one of the roundabout phrases in which the Chinese delight to express painful or repulsive subjects. No emperor ever "dies," he becomes "a guest on high." No son will say that his parents are "dead;" but merely that "they are not." The death of an official is expressed by "he is drawing no salary;" of an ordinary man it may be said that "he has become an ancient," very much in the same way that we say "he has joined the majority." A corpse in a coffin is in its "long home;" when buried, it is in "the city of old age," or on "the terrace of night." To say grossly, then, that a man took poison would be an offence to ears polite.

CHAPTER VIII

RECREATION

To return, after a long digression. The age of manly sport, as above described, has long passed away; and the only hope is for a revival under the changing conditions of modern China. Some few athletic exercises have survived; and until recently, archery, in which the Tartars have always excelled, was regarded almost as a semi-divine accomplishment. Kite-flying has reached a high level of skill. Clever little "messengers" have been devised, which run up the string, carrying fire-crackers which explode at a great height. There is a game of shuttlecock, without the battledore, for which the feet are used as a substitute; and "diavolo," recently introduced into Europe, is an ancient Chinese pastime. A few Manchus, too, may be seen skating during the long northern winter, but the modern inhabitant of the Flowery Land, be he Manchu or Chinese, much prefers an indoor game to anything else, especially when, as is universally the case, a stake of money is involved.

Gambling is indeed a very marked feature of Chinese life. A child buying a cake will often go double or quits with the stall-keeper, to see if he is to have two cakes or nothing, the question being settled by a throw of dice in a bowl. Of the interval allowed for meals, a gang of coolies will devote a portion to a game of cards. The cards used are smaller than the European pack, and of course differently marked; they were the invention of a lady of the Palace in the tenth century, who substituted imitation leaves of gilt paper for real leaves, which had previously been adopted for playing some kind of game. There are also various games played with chequers, some of great antiquity; and there is chess, that is to say, a game so little differing from our chess as to leave no doubt as to the common origin of both. In all of these the money element comes in; and it is not too much to say that more homes are broken up, and more misery caused by this truly national vice than can be attributed to any other cause.

For pleasure pure and simple, independent of gains and losses, the theatre occupies the warmest place in every Chinaman's heart. If gambling is a national vice in China, the drama must be set off as the national recreation. Life would be unthinkable to the vast majority if its monotony were not broken by the periodical performance of stage-plays. It is from this source that a certain familiarity with the great historical episodes of the past may be pleasantly picked up over a pipe and a cup of tea; while the farce, occasionally perhaps erring on the side of breadth, affords plenty of merriment to the laughter-loving crowd.

Ability to make Chinamen laugh is a great asset; and a foreigner who carries this about with him will find it stand him in much better stead than a revolver. When, many years ago, a vessel was wrecked on the coast of Formosa, the crew and passengers were at once seized, and confined for some time in a building, where traces of their inscriptions could be seen up to quite a recent date. At length, they were all taken out for execution; but before the ghastly order was carried out, one of the number so amused everybody by cutting capers and turning head over heels, that the presiding mandarin said he was a funny fellow, and positively allowed him to escape.

With regard to the farce itself, it is not so much the actual wit of the dialogue which carries away the audience as the refined skill of the actor, who has to pass through many trials before he is considered to be fit for the stage. Beginning as quite a boy, in addition to committing to memory a large number of plays—not merely his own part, but the whole play—he has to undergo a severe physical training, part of which consists in standing for an hour every day with his mouth wide open, to inhale the morning air. He is taught to sing, to walk, to strut, and to perform a variety of gymnastic exercises, such as standing on his head, or turning somersaults. His first classification is as male or female actor, no women having been allowed to perform since the days of the Emperor Ch'ien Lung (A.D. 1736-1796), whose mother was an actress, just as in Shakespeare's time the parts for women were always taken by young men or boys. When once this is settled, it only remains to enrol him as tragedian, comedian, low-comedy actor, walking gentleman or lady, and similar parts, according to his capabilities.

It is not too much to say that women are very little missed on the Chinese stage. The make-up of the actor is so perfect, and his imitation of the feminine voice and manner, down to the smallest detail, even to the small feet, is so exact in every point, that he would be a clever observer who could positively detect impersonation by a man.

Generally speaking, a Chinese actor has many more difficulties to face than his colleague in the West. In addition to the expression of all shades of feeling, from mirth to melancholy, the former has to keep up a perpetual make-believe in another sense, which is further great strain upon his nerves. There being no scenery, no furniture, and no appointments of any except the slenderest kind upon the stage, he has to create in the minds of his audience a belief that all these missing accessories are nevertheless before their eyes. A general comes upon the scene, with a whip in his hand, and a studied movement not only suggests that he is dismounting from a horse, but outlines the animal itself. In the same manner, he remounts and rides off again; while some other actor speaks from the top of a small table, which is forthwith transfigured, and becomes to all intents and purposes a castle.

Many of those who might be apt to smile at the simple Chinese mind which can tolerate such absurdities in the way of make-believe, require to be reminded that the stage in the days of Queen Elizabeth was worked on very much the same lines. Sir Philip Sidney tells us that the scene of an imagined garden with imagined flowers had to do duty at one time for an imagined shipwreck, and at another for an imagined battlefield, the spectator in the latter case being helped out by two opposing soldiers armed with swords and bucklers. Even Shakespeare, in the Prologue to his play of *Henry V*, speaks of imagining one man to be an army of a thousand, and says:—

> Think, when we talk of horses that you see them
> Printing their proud hoofs i' the receiving earth;
> For 'tis your thoughts that now must deck our kings.

Here, then, is good authority for the quaint system that still prevails in China.

Hundreds of Chinese pilgrims annually went their weary way to the top of Mount Omi in the province of Ssuch'uan, and gaze downward from a sheer and lofty precipice to view a huge circular belt of light, which is called the Glory of Buddha. Some see it, some do not; the Chinese say that the whole thing is a question of faith. In a somewhat similar sense, the dramatic enthusiast sees before him such beings of the mind as the genuine actor is able to call up. The Philistine cannot reach this pitch; but he is sharp enough to see other things which to the eye of the sympathetic spectator are absolutely non-existent. Some of the latter will be enumerated below.

The Chinese stage has no curtain; and the orchestra is on the stage itself, behind the actors. There is no prompter and no call-boy. Stage footmen wait at the sides to carry in screens, small tables, and an odd chair or two, to represent houses, city walls, and so on, or hand cups of tea to the actors when their throats become dry from vociferous singing, which is always in falsetto. All this in the face of the audience. Dead people get up and walk off the stage; or while lying dead, contrive to alter their facial expression, and then get up and carry themselves off. There is no interval between one play and the next following, which probably gives rise to the erroneous belief that Chinese plays are long, the fact being that they are very short. According to the Penal Code, there may be no impersonation of emperors and empresses of past ages, but this clause is now held to refer solely to the present dynasty.

For the man in the street and his children, there are to be seen everywhere in China where a sufficient number of people gather together, Punch-and-Judy shows of quite a high class in point of skill and general attractiveness. These shows are variously traced back to the eighth and second centuries B.C., and to the seventh century A.D., even the latest of which periods would considerably antedate the appearance of performing marionettes in this country or on the Continent. Associated with the second century B.C., the story runs that the Emperor of the day was closely besieged by a terrible Hun chieftain, who was accompanied by his wife. It occurred to one of his Majesty's staff to exhibit on the walls of the town, in full view of the enemy, a number of manikins, dressed up to a deceptive resemblance to beautiful girls. The wife of the Hun chieftain then persuaded her husband to draw off his forces, and the Emperor escaped.

By the Chinese marionettes, little plays on familiar subjects are performed; many are of a more serious turn than the loves of Mr. Punch, while others again are of the knock-about style so dear to the ordinary boy and girl. Besides such entertainments as these, the streets of a Chinese city offer other shows to those who desire to be amused. An acrobat, a rope-dancer or a conjurer will take up a pitch right in the middle of the roadway, and the traffic has to get on as best it can. A theatrical stage will sometimes completely block a street, and even foot-passengers will have to find their way round. There is also the public story-reader, who for his own sake will choose a convenient spot near to some busy thoroughfare; and there, to an assembled crowd, he will read out, not in the difficult book-language, but in the colloquial dialect of the place, stories of war and heroism, soldiers led to night-attacks with wooden bits in their mouths to prevent them from talking in the ranks, the victory of the loyal and the rout and slaughter of the rebel. Or it may be a tale of giants, goblins and wizards; the bewitching of promising young men by lovely maidens who turn out to be really foxes in disguise, ending as usual in the triumph of virtue and the discomfiture of vice. The fixed eyes and open mouths of the crowd, listening with rapt attention, is a sight which, once seen, is not easily forgotten.

For the ordinary man, China is simply peopled with bogies and devils, the spirits of the wicked or of those unfortunate enough not to secure decent burial with all its accompanying worship and rites. These creatures, whose bodies cast no shadow, lurk in dark corners, ready to pounce on some unwary passer-by and possibly tear out his heart. Many a Confucianist, sturdy in his faith that "devils only exist for those who believe in them," will hesitate to visit by night a lonely spot, or even to enter a disused tumbledown building by day. Some of the stories told are certainly well fitted to make a deep impression upon young and highly-strung nerves. For instance, one man who was too fond of the bottle placed some liquor alongside his bed, to be drunk during the night. On stretching out his hand to reach the flask, he was seized by a demon, and dragged gradually into the earth. In response to his shrieks, his relatives and neighbors only arrived in time to see the ground close over his head, just as though he had fallen into water.

From this story it will be rightly gathered that the Chinese mostly sleep on the ground floor. In Peking, houses of more than one storey are absolutely barred; the reason being that each house is built round a courtyard, which usually has trees in it, and in which the ladies of the establishment delight to sit and sew, and take the air and all the exercise they can manage to get.

Another blood-curdling story is that of four travelers who arrived by night at an inn, but could obtain no other accommodation than a room in which was lying the corpse of the landlord's daughter-in-law. Three of the four were soon snoring; the fourth, however, remained awake, and very soon heard a creaking of the trestles on which was the dead body dressed out in paper robes, ready for burial. To his horror he saw the girl get up, and go and breathe on his companions; so by the time she came to him he had his head tucked well under the bedclothes. After a little while he kicked one of the others; but finding that his friend did not move, he suddenly grabbed his own trousers and made a bolt for the door. In a moment the corpse was up and after him, following him down the street, and gaining gradually on him, no one coming to the rescue in spite of his loud shrieks as he ran. So he slipped behind a tree, and dodged right and left, the infuriated corpse also dodging right and left, and making violent efforts to get him. At length, the girl made a rush forward with one arm on each side, in the hope of thus grabbing her victim. The traveler, however, fell backwards and escaped her clutch, while she remained rigidly embracing the tree. By and by he was found senseless on the ground; and the corpse was removed from the tree, but with great difficulty, as the fingers were buried in the bark so deep that the nails were not even visible. The other three travelers were found dead in their beds.

Periodical feasting may be regarded as another form of amusement by which the Chinese seek to relieve the monotony of life. They have never reserved one day in seven for absolute rest, though of late years Chinese merchants connected with foreign trade have to some extent fallen in with the observance of Sunday. Quite a number of days during the year are set apart as public holidays, but no one is obliged to keep them as such, unless he likes, with one important exception. The festival of the New Year cannot be ignored by any one. For about ten days before this date, and twenty days after it, the public offices are closed and no business is transacted, the seal of each official is handed over for safe keeping to the official's wife, a fact which helps to dispose of the libel that women in China are the down-trodden creatures they are often represented to be. All debts have to be paid and accounts squared by midnight on the last day of the old year. A few nights previously, offerings of an excessively sticky sweetmeat are made to the Spirit of the Hearth, one of whose functions is that of an accusing angel. The Spirit is then on the point of starting for his annual visit to heaven, and lest any of the disclosures he might make should entail unpleasant consequences, it is adjudged best that he shall be rendered incapable of making any disclosures at all. The unwary god finds his lips tightly glued together, and is unable to utter a single word. Meanwhile, fire-crackers are being everywhere let off on a colossal scale, the object being to frighten away the evil spirits which have collected during the past twelve months, and to begin the year afresh. The day itself is devoted to calling, in one's best clothes, on relatives, friends and official superiors, for all of whom it is customary to leave a present. The relatives and friends receive "wet" gifts, such as fruit or cakes; officials also receive wet gifts, but underneath the top layer will be found something "dry," in the shape of silver or bank-notes. Everybody salutes everybody with the conventional saying, "New joy, new joy; get rich, get rich!" Yet here again, as in all things Chinese, we find a striking exception to this good-natured rule. No one says "Get rich, get rich!" to the undertaker.

A high authority (on other matters) has recently stated that the Chinese calendar "begins just when the Emperor chooses to say it shall. He is like the captain of a ship, who says of the hour, 'Make it so,' and it is so." The truth is that New Year's Day is determined by the Astronomical Board, according to fixed rules, just as Easter is determined; and it may fall on any day between the 21st of January and the 20th of February, but neither before the former date nor after the latter date, in spite even of the most threatening orders from the Palace. This book will indeed have been written in vain if the reader lays it down without having realized that no such wanton interference on the part of their rulers would be tolerated by the Chinese people. But we are wandering away from merry-making and festivity.

In their daily life the Chinese are extremely moderate eaters and mostly tea-drinkers, even the wealthy confining themselves to few and simple dishes of pork, fowl, or fish, with the ever-present accompaniment of rice. The puppy-dog, on which the people are popularly believed to live, as the French on frogs, is a stall-fed animal, and has always been, and still is, an article of food; but the consumption of dog-flesh is really very restricted, and many thousands of Chinamen have never tasted dog in their lives. According to the popular classification of foods, those who live on vegetables get strong, those who live on meat become brave, those who live on grain acquire wisdom, and those who live on air become divine.

At banquets the scene changes, and course after course of curiously compounded and highly spiced dishes, cooked as only Chinese cooks know how, are placed before the guests. The wine, too, goes merrily round; bumpers are drunk at short intervals, and the wine-cups are held upside down, to show that there are no heel-taps. Forfeits are exacted over the game of "guess-fingers," for failure to cap a verse, or for any other equally sufficient (or insufficient) reason; and the penalty is an extra bumper for the loser.

This lively picture requires, perhaps, a little further explanation. Chinese "wine" is an ardent spirit distilled from rice, and is modified in various ways so as to produce

102

certain brands, some of which are of quite moderate strength, and really may be classed as wine. It is always drunk hot, the heat being supplied by vessels of boiling water, in which the pewter wine-flasks are kept standing. The wine-cups are small, and it is possible to drink a good many of them without feeling in the least overcome. Even so, many diners now refuse to touch wine at all, the excuse always being that it flushes the face uncomfortably. Perhaps they fear an undeserved imputation of drunkenness, remembering their own cynical saying: "A bottle-nosed man may be a tee-totaller, but no one will believe it." To judge from their histories and their poetry, the Chinese seem once upon a time to have been a fairly tipsy nation: now-a-days, the truth lies the other way. An official who died A.D. 639, and was the originator of epitaphs in China, wrote his own, as follows:—

Fu I loved the green hills and white clouds . . .
Alas! he died of drink!

There are exceptions, no doubt, as to every rule in every country; but such sights as drunken men tumbling about the streets, or lying senseless by the roadside, are not to be seen in China. "It is not wine," says the proverb, "which makes a man drunk; it is the man himself."

Even at banquets, which are often very rich and costly, unnecessary expense is by no means encouraged. Dishes of fruit, of a kind which no one would wish to eat, and which are placed on the table for show or ornament, are simply clever imitations in painted wood, and pass from banquet to banquet as part of the ordinary paraphernalia of a feast; no one is deceived. The same form of open and above-board deception appears in many other ways. There are societies organized for visiting in a comfortable style of pilgrimage some famous mountain of historic interest. Names are put down, and money is collected; and then the party starts off by boat or in sedan-chairs, as the case may be. On arriving at the mountain, there is a grand feast, and after the picnic, for such it is, every one goes home again. That is the real thing; now for the imitation. Names are put down, and money is collected, as before; but the funds are spent over a feast at home, alongside of a paper mountain.

Another of these deceptions, which deceive nobody, is one which might be usefully adapted to life in other countries. A Chinaman meeting in the street a friend, and having no leisure to stop and talk, or perhaps meeting some one with whom he may be unwilling to talk, will promptly put up his open fan to screen his face, and pass on. The suggestion is that, wishing to pass without notice, he fails to see the person in question, and it would be a serious breach of decorum on the part of the latter to ignore the hint thus conveyed.

Japan, who may be said to have borrowed the civilization of China, lock, stock and barrel—her literature, her moral code, her arts, her sciences, her manners and customs, her ceremonial, and even her national dress—invented the folding fan, which in the early part of the fifteenth century formed part of the tribute sent from Korea to Peking, and even later was looked upon by the Chinese as quite a curiosity. In the early ages, fans were made of feathers, as still at the present day; but the more modern fan of native origin is a light frame of bamboo, wood or ivory, round or otherwise, over which silk is stretched, offering a convenient medium for the inscription of poems, or for paintings, as exchanged between friend and friend.

The same innocent form of deception, which deceives nobody, is carried out when two officials, seated in sedan-chairs, have to pass one another. If they are of about equal rank, etiquette demands that they should alight from their chairs, and perform mutual salutations. To obviate the extreme inconvenience of this rule, large wooden fans are carried in all processions of the kind, and these are hastily thrust between the passing officials, so that neither becomes aware of the other's existence on the scene. The case is different when one of the two is of higher rank. The official of inferior grade is bound to stop and get out of his chair while his superior passes by, though even now he has a chance of escape; he hears the gong beaten to clear the way for the great man, whose rank he can tell from the number of consecutive blows given; and hurriedly turns off down a side street.

An historical instance of substituting the shadow for the reality is that of the great general Ts'ao Ts'ao, third century A.D., who for some breach of the law sentenced himself to death, but satisfied his sense of justice by cutting off his hair. An emperor of the sixth century, who was a devout Buddhist, and therefore unable to countenance any destruction of life, had all the sacrificial animals made of dough.

The opium question, which will claim a few words later on, has been exhaustively threshed out; and in view of the contradictory statements for and against the habit of opium smoking, it is recognized that any conclusion, satisfactory to both parties, is a very remote possibility. The Chinese themselves, who are chiefly interested in the argument, have lately come to a very definite conclusion, which is that opium has to go; and it seems that in spite of almost invincible obstacles, the sincerity and patriotism which are being infused into the movement will certainly, sooner or later, achieve the desired end. It is perhaps worth noting that in the Decree of 1906, which ordered the abolition of opium smoking, the old Empress Dowager, who was herself over sixty and a moderate smoker, inserted a clause excusing from the operation of the new law all persons already more than sixty years of age.

CHAPTER IX

THE MONGOLS, 1260-1368

Lack of patriotism is often hurled by foreigners as a reproach to the Chinese. The charge cannot be substantiated, any more than it could be if directed against some nation in Europe. If willingness to sacrifice everything, including life itself, may be taken as a fair test of genuine patriotism, then it will be found, if historical records be not ignored, that China has furnished numberless brilliant examples of true patriots who chose to die rather than suffer dishonor to themselves or to their country. A single instance must suffice.

The time is the close of the thirteenth century, when the Mongols under Kublai Khan were steadily dispossessing the once glorious and powerful House of Sung, and placing the empire of China under alien rule. Disaster followed disaster, until almost the last army of the Sungs was cut to pieces, and the famous statesman and general in command, Wen (pronounced *One*) T'ien-hsian, fell into the hands of the Mongols. He was ordered, but refused, to write and advise capitulation, and every effort was subsequently made to induce him to own allegiance to the conquerors. He was kept in prison for three years. "My dungeon," he wrote, "is lighted by the will-o'-the-wisp alone; no breath of spring cheers the murky solitude in which I dwell. Exposed to mist and dew, I had many times thought to die; and yet, through the seasons of two revolving years, disease hovered around me in vain. The dank, unhealthy soil to me became Paradise itself. For there was that within me which misfortune could not steal away; and so I remained firm, gazing at the white clouds floating over my head, and bearing in my heart a sorrow boundless as the sky."

At length he was summoned into the presence of Kublai Khan, who said to him, "What is it you want?" "By the grace of the Sung Emperor," he replied, "I became His Majesty's Minister. I cannot serve two masters. I only ask to die." Accordingly, he was executed, meeting his death with composure, and making an obeisance in the direction of the old capital. His last words were, "My work is finished." Compare this with the quiet death-bed of another statesman, who flourished in the previous century. He had advised an enormous cession of territory to the Tartars, and had brought about the execution of a patriot soldier, who wished to recover it at all costs. He was loaded with honors, and on the very night he died he was raised to the rank of Prince. He was even canonized, after the usual custom, as Loyalty Manifested, on a mistaken estimate of his career; but fifty years later his title was changed to False and Foul and his honors were cancelled, while the people at large took his degraded name for use as an alternative to spittoon.

Two names of quite recent patriots deserve to be recorded here as a tribute to their earnest devotion to the real interests of their country, and incidentally for the far-reaching consequences of their heroic act, which probably saved the lives of many foreigners in various parts of China. It was during the Boxer troubles in Peking, at the beginning of the siege of the legations, that Yuan Ch'ang and Hsu Ching-ch'eng, two high Chinese officials, ventured to memorialize the Empress Dowager upon the fatal policy, and even criminality, of the whole proceedings, imploring her Majesty at a meeting of the Grand Council to reconsider her intention of issuing orders for the extermination of all foreigners. In spite of their remonstrances, a decree was issued to that effect and forwarded to the high authorities of the various provinces; but it failed to accomplish what had been intended, for these two heroes, taking their lives in their hands, had altered the words "slay all foreigners" into "protect all foreigners." Some five to six weeks later, when the siege was drawing to a close, the alteration was discovered; and next day those two men were hurriedly beheaded, meeting death with such firmness and fortitude as only true patriotism could inspire.

The Mongols found it no easy task to dispossess the House of Sung, which had many warm adherents to its cause. It was in 1206 that Genghis Khan began to make arrangements for a projected invasion of China, and by 1214 he was master of all the enemy's territory north of the Yellow River, except Peking. He then made peace with the Golden Tartar emperor of northern China; but his suspicions were soon aroused, and hostilities were renewed. In 1227 he died, while conducting a campaign in Central Asia; and it remained for his vigorous grandson, Kublai Khan, to complete the conquest of China more than half a century afterwards. So early as 1260, Kublai was able to proclaim himself emperor at Xanadu, which means Imperial Capital, and lay about one hundred and eighty miles north of modern Peking, where, in those days known as Khan-baligh (Marco Polo's Cambaluc), he established himself four years later; but twenty years of severe fighting had still to pass away before the empire was finally subdued. The Sung troops were gradually driven south, contesting every inch of ground with a dogged resistance born of patriotic Endeavour. In 1278 Canton was taken, and the heroic Wen T'ien-hsiang was captured through the treachery of a subordinate. In 1279 the last stronghold of the Sungs was beleaguered by land and sea. Shut up in their ships which they formed into a compact mass and fortified with towers and breastworks, the patriots, deprived of fresh water, harassed by attacks during the day and by fire-ships at night, maintained the unequal struggle for a month. But when, after a hard day's fighting, the Sung commander found himself left with only sixteen vessels, he fled up a creek. His retreat was cut off; and then at length despairing of his country, he bade his wife and children throw themselves overboard. He himself, taking the young emperor on his back, followed their example, and thus brought the great Sung dynasty to an end.

The grandeur of Kublai Khan's reign may be gathered from the pages of Marco Polo, in which, too, allusion is made to Bayan, the skilful general to whom so much of the military success of the Mongols was due. Korea, Burma, and Annam became dependencies of China, and continued to send tribute as such even up to quite modern times. Hardly so successful was Kublai Khan's huge naval expedition against Japan, which, in point of number of ships and men, the insular character of the enemy's country, the chastisement intended, and the total loss of the fleet in a storm, aided by the stubborn resistance offered by the Japanese themselves—suggests a very obvious comparison with the object and fate of the Spanish Armada.

Among the more peaceful developments of Mongol rule at this epoch may be mentioned the introduction of a written character for the Mongol language. It was the work of a Tibetan priest, named Baschpa, and was based upon the written language of a nation known as the Ouigours (akin to the Turks), which had in turn been based upon Syraic, and is written in vertical lines connected by ligatures. Similarly, until 1599 there was no written Manchu language; a script, based upon the Mongol, was then devised, also in vertical lines or columns like Chinese, but read from left to right.

Under Kublai Khan the calendar was revised, and the Imperial Academy was opened; the Yellow River was explored to its source, and bank-notes were made current. The Emperor himself was an ardent Buddhist, but he took care that proper honors were paid to Confucius; on the other hand, he issued orders that all Taoist literature of the baser kind was to be destroyed. Behind all this there was extortionate taxation, a form of oppression the Chinese have never learned to tolerate, and discontent led to disorder. Kublai's grandson was for a time an honest ruler and tried to stem the tide, but by 1368 the mandate of the Mongols was exhausted. They were an alien race, and the Chinese were glad to get rid of them.

Chinese soldiers are often stigmatized as arrant cowards, who run away at the slightest provocation, their first thought being for the safety of their own skins. No doubt Chinese soldiers do run away—sometimes; at other times they fight to the death, as has been amply proved over and over again. It is the old story of marking the hits and not the misses. A great deal depends upon sufficiency and regularity of pay. Soldiers with pay in arrear, half clad, hungry, and ill armed, as has frequently been the case in Chinese campaigns, cannot be expected to do much for the flag. Given the reverse of these conditions, things would be likely to go badly with the enemy, whosoever he might be.

Underneath a mask of complete facial stolidity, the Chinese conceal one of the most excitable temperaments to be found in any race, as will soon be discovered by watching an ordinary street row between a couple of men, or still better, women. A Chinese crowd of men—women keep away—is a good-tempered and orderly mob, partly because not inflamed by drink, when out to enjoy the Feast of the Lanterns, or to watch the twinkling lamps float down a river to light the wandering ghosts of the drowned on the night of their All Souls' Day, sacred to the memory of the dead; but a rumor, a mere whisper, the more baseless often the more potent, will transform these law-abiding people into a crowd of fiends. In times when popular feeling runs high, as when large numbers of men were said to be deprived suddenly and mysteriously of their queues, or when the word went round, as it has done on more occasions than one, that foreigners were kidnapping children in order to use their eyes for medicine,—in such times the masses, incited by those who ought to know better, get completely out of hand.

A curious and tragic instance of this excitability occurred some years ago. The viceroy of a province had succeeded in organizing a contingent of foreign-drilled troops, under the guidance and leadership of two qualified foreign instructors. After some time had elapsed, and it was thought that the troops were sufficiently trained to make a good show, it was arranged that a sham fight should be held in the presence of the viceroy himself. The men were divided into two bodies under the two foreign commanders, and in the course of operations one body had to defend a village, while the other had to attack it. When the time came to capture the village at the point of the bayonet, both sides lost their heads; there was a fierce hand-to-hand fight in stern reality, and before this could be effectively stopped four men had been killed outright and sixteen badly wounded.

Considering how squalid many Chinese homes are, it is all the more astonishing to find such deep attachment to them. There exists in the language a definite word for *home*, in its fullest English sense. As a written character, it is supposed to picture the idea of a family, the component parts being a "roof" with "three persons" underneath. There is, indeed, another and more fanciful explanation of this character, namely, that it is composed of a "roof" with a "pig" underneath, the forms for "three men" and "pig" being sufficiently alike at any rate to justify the suggestion. This analysis would not be altogether out of place in China any more than in Ireland; but as a matter of fact the balance of evidence is in favor of the "three men," which number, it may be remarked, is that which technically constitutes a crowd.

Whatever may be the literary view of the word "home," it is quite certain that to the ordinary Chinaman there is no place like it. "One mile away from home is not so good as being in it," says a proverb with a punning turn which cannot be brought out in English. Another says, "Every day is happy at home, every moment miserable abroad." It may therefore be profitable to look inside a Chinese home, if only to discover wherein its attractiveness lies.

All such homes are arranged more or less on the patriarchal system; that is to say, at the head of the establishment are a father and mother, who rank equally so far as their juniors are concerned; the mother receiving precisely the same share of deference in life, and of ancestral worship after death, as the father. The children grow up; wives are sought for the boys, and husbands for the girls, at about the ages of eighteen and sixteen, respectively. The former bring their wives into the paternal home; the latter belong, from the day of their marriage, to the paternal homes of their husbands. Bachelors and old maids have no place in the Chinese scheme of life. Theoretically, bride and bridegroom are not supposed to see each other until the wedding-day, when the girl's veil is lifted on her arrival at her father-in-law's house; in practice, the young people usually manage to get at least a glimpse of one another, usually with the connivance of their elders. Thus the family expands, and one of the greatest happinesses which can befall a Chinaman is to have "five generations in the hall." Owing to early marriage, this is not nearly so uncommon as it is in Western countries. There is an authentic record of an old statesman who had so many descendants that when they came to congratulate him on his birthdays, he was quite unable to remember all their names, and could only bow as they passed in line before him.

As to income and expenditure, the earnings of the various members go into a common purse, out of which expenses are paid. Every one has a right to food and shelter; and so it is that if some are out of work, the strain is not individually felt; they take their rations as usual. On the death of the father, it is not at all uncommon for the mother to take up the reins, though it is more usual for the eldest son to take his place. Sometimes, after the death of the mother—and then it is accounted a bad day for the family fortunes—the brothers cannot agree; the property is divided, and each son sets up for himself, a proceeding which is forbidden by the Penal Code during the parents' lifetime. Meanwhile, any member of the family who should disgrace himself in any way, as by becoming an inveterate gambler and permanently neglecting his work, or by developing the opium vice to great excess, would be formally cast out, his name being struck off the ancestral register. Men of this stamp generally sink lower and lower, until they swell the ranks of professional beggars, to die perhaps in a ditch; but such cases are happily of rare occurrence.

In the ordinary peaceful family, regulated according to Confucian principles of filial piety, fraternal love, and loyalty to the sovereign, we find love of home exalted to a passion; and bitter is the day of leave-taking for a long absence, as when a successful son starts to take up his official appointment at a distant post. The latter, not being able to hold office in his native province, may have a long and sometimes dangerous journey to make, possibly to the other end of the empire. In any case, years must elapse before he can revisit "the mulberry and the elm"— the garden he leaves behind. He may take his "old woman" and family with him, or they may follow later on; as another alternative, the "old woman" with the children may remain permanently in the ancestral home, while the husband carries on his official career alone. Under such circumstances as the last-mentioned, no one, including his own wife, is shocked if he consoles himself with a "small old woman," whom he picks up at his new place of abode. The "small old woman" is indeed often introduced into families where the "principal old woman" fails to contribute the first of "the three blessings of which every one desires to have plenty," namely, sons, money, and life. Instances are not uncommon of the wife herself urging this course upon her husband; and but for this system the family line would often come to an end, failing recourse to another system, namely, adoption, which is also brought into play when all hope of a lineal descendant is abandoned.

Whether she has children or not, the principal wife—the only wife, in fact—never loses her supremacy as the head of the household. The late Empress Dowager was originally a concubine; by virtue of motherhood she was raised to the rank of Western Empress, but never legitimately took precedence of the wife, whose superiority was indicated by her title of Eastern Empress, the east being more honorable than the west. The emperor always sits with his face towards the south.

The story of Sung Hung, a statesman who flourished about the time of the Christian era, pleasantly illustrates a chivalrous side of the Chinese character. This man raised himself from a humble station in life to be a minister of state, and was subsequently ennobled as marquis. The emperor then wished him to put away his wife, who was a woman of the people, and marry a princess; to which he nobly replied: "Sire, the partner of my porridge days shall never go down from my hall."

Of the miseries of exile from the ancestral home, lurid pictures have been drawn by many poets and others. One man, ordered from some soft southern climate to a post in the colder north, will complain that the spring with its flowers is too late in arriving; another "cannot stand the water and earth," by which is meant that the climate does not agree with him; a third is satisfied with his surroundings, but is still a constant sufferer from home-sickness. Such a one was the poet who wrote the following lines:—

Away to the east lie fair forests of trees,
From the flowers on the west comes a scent-laden breeze,
Yet my eyes daily turn to my far-away home,
Beyond the broad river, its waves and its foam.

114

And such, too, is the note of innumerable songs in exile, written for the most part by officials stationed in distant parts of the empire; sometimes by exiles in a harsher sense, namely, those persons who have been banished to the frontier for disaffection, maladministration of government, and like offences. A bright particular gem in Chinese literature, referring to love of home, was the work of a young poet who received an appointment as magistrate, but threw it up after a tenure of only eighty-three days, declaring that he could not "crook the hinges of his back for five pecks of rice a day," that being the regulation pay of his office. It was written to celebrate his own return, and runs as follows:—

"Homewards I bend my steps. My fields, my gardens, are choked with weeds: should I not go? My soul has led a bondsman's life: why should I remain to pine? But I will waste no grief upon the past: I will devote my energies to the future. I have not wandered far astray. I feel that I am on the right track once again.

"Lightly, lightly, speeds my boat along, my garments fluttering to the gentle breeze. I inquire my route as I go. I grudge the slowness of the dawning day. From afar I descry by old home, and joyfully press onwards in my haste. The servants rush forth to meet me: my children cluster at the gate. The place is a wilderness; but there is the old pine-tree and my chrysanthemums. I take the little ones by the hand, and pass in. Wine is brought in full bottles, and I pour out in brimming cups. I gaze out at my favorite branches. I loll against the window in my new-found freedom. I look at the sweet children on my knee.

"And now I take my pleasure in my garden. There is a gate, but it is rarely opened. I lean on my staff as I wander about or sit down to rest. I raise my head and contemplate the lovely scene. Clouds rise, unwilling, from the bottom of the hills: the weary bird seeks its nest again. Shadows vanish, but still I linger round my lonely pine. Home once more! I'll have no friendships to distract me hence. The times are out of joint for me; and what have I to seek from men? In the pure enjoyment of the family circle I will pass my days, cheering my idle hours with lute and book. My husbandmen will tell me when spring-time is nigh, and when there will be work in the furrowed fields. Thither I shall repair by cart or by boat, through the deep gorge, over the dizzy cliff, trees bursting merrily into leaf, the streamlet swelling from its tiny source. Glad is this renewal of life in due season: but for me, I rejoice that my journey is over. Ah, how short a time it is that we are here! Why, then, not set our hearts at rest, ceasing to trouble whether we remain or go? What boots it to wear out the soul with anxious thoughts? I want not wealth: I want not power: heaven is beyond my hopes. Then let me stroll through the bright hours, as they pass, in my garden among my flowers; or I will mount the hill and sing my song, or weave my verse beside the limpid brook. Thus will I work out my allotted span, content with the appointments of Fate, my spirit free from care."

Besides contributing a large amount of beautiful poetry, this author provided his own funeral oration, the earliest which has come down to us, written just before his death in A.D. 427. Funeral orations are not only pronounced by some friend at the grave, but are further solemnly consumed by fire, in the belief that they will thus reach the world of spirits, and be a joy and an honour to the deceased, in the same sense that paper houses, horses, sedan-chairs, and similar articles, are burnt for the use of the dead.

CHAPTER X

MINGS AND CH'INGS, 1368-1911

The first half of the fourteenth century, which witnessed the gradual decline of Mongol influence and power, was further marked by the birth of a humble individual destined to achieve a new departure in the history of the empire. At the age of seventeen, Chu Yuan-chang lost both his parents and an elder brother. It was a year of famine, and they died from want of food. He had no money to buy coffins, and was forced to bury them in straw. He then, as a last resource, decided to enter the Buddhist priesthood, and accordingly enrolled himself as a novice; but together with the other novices, he was soon dismissed, the priests being unable to provide even for their own wants. After this he wandered about, and finally joined a party of rebels commanded by one of his own uncles. Rapidly rising to the highest military rank, he gradually found himself at the head of a huge army, and by 1368 was master of so many provinces that he proclaimed himself first emperor of the Great Ming dynasty, under the title of Hung (*Hoong*) Wu, and fixed his capital at Nanking. In addition to his military genius, he showed almost equal skill in the administration of the empire, and also became a liberal patron of literature and education. He organized the present system of examinations, now in a transition state; restored the native Chinese style of dress as worn under the T'ang dynasty, which is still the costume seen on the stage; published a Penal Code of mitigated severity; drew up a kind of Domesday Book under which taxation was regulated; and fixed the coinage upon a proper basis,

117

government notes and copper *cash* being equally current. Eunuchs were prohibited from holding official posts, and Buddhism and Taoism were both made state religions.

This truly great monarch died in 1398, and was succeeded by a grandson, whose very receding forehead had been a source of much annoyance to his grandfather, though the boy grew up clever and could make good verses. The first act of this new emperor was to dispossess his uncles of various important posts held by them; but this was not tolerated by one of them, who had already made himself conspicuous by his talents, and he promptly threw off his allegiance. In the war which ensued, victory attended his arms throughout, and at length he entered Nanking, the capital, in triumph. And now begins one of those romantic episodes which from time to time lend an unusual interest to the dry bones of Chinese history. In the confusion which followed upon the entry of troops into his palace, the young and defeated emperor vanished, and was never seen again; although in after years pretenders started up on more than one occasion, and obtained the support of many in their efforts to recover the throne. It is supposed that the fugitive made his way to the distant province of Yunnan in the garb of a Buddhist priest, left to him, so the story runs, by his grandfather. After nearly forty years of wandering, he is said to have gone to Peking and to have lived in seclusion in the palace there until his death. He was recognized by a eunuch from a mole on his left foot, but the eunuch was afraid to reveal his identity.

The victorious uncle mounted the throne in the year 1403, under the now famous title of Yung Lo (*Yoong Law*), and soon showed that he could govern as well as he could fight. He brought immigrants from populous provinces to repeople the districts which had been laid waste by war. Peking was built, and in 1421 the seat of government was transferred thither, where it has remained ever since. A new Penal Code was drawn up. Various military expeditions were despatched against the Tartars, and missions under the charge of eunuchs were sent to Java,

Sumatra, Siam, and even reached Ceylon and the Red Sea. The day of doubt in regard to the general accuracy of Chinese annals has gone by; were it otherwise, a recent (1911) discovery in Ceylon would tend to dispel suspicion on one point. A tablet has just been unearthed at Galle, bearing an inscription in Arabic, Chinese and Tamil. The Arabic is beyond decipherment, but enough is left of the Chinese to show that the tablet was erected in 1409 to commemorate a visit by the eunuch Cheng Ho, who passed several times backwards and forwards over that route. In 1411 the same eunuch was sent as envoy to Japan, and narrowly escaped with his life.

The emperor was a warm patron of literature, and succeeded in bringing about the achievement of the most gigantic literary task that the world has ever seen. He employed a huge staff of scholars to compile an encyclopaedia which should contain within the compass of a single work all that had ever been written in the four departments of (1) the Confucian Canon, (2) history, (3) philosophy, and (4) general literature, including astronomy, geography, cosmogony, medicine, divination, Buddhism, Taoism, handicrafts and arts. The completed work, over which a small army of scholars—more than two thousand in all—had spent five years, ran to no fewer than 22,877 sections, to which must be added an index occupying 60 sections. The whole was bound up (Chinese style) in 11,000 volumes, averaging over half-an-inch in thickness, and measuring one foot eight inches in length by one foot in breadth. Thus, if all these were laid flat one upon another, the column so formed would rise considerably higher than the very top of St. Paul's. Further, each section contains about twenty leaves, making a total of 917,480 pages for the whole work, with a grand total of 366,000,000 words. Taking 100 Chinese words as the equivalent of 130 English, due to the greater condensation of Chinese literary style, it will be found that even the mighty river of the *Encyclopedia Britannica* "shrinks to a rill" when compared with this overwhelming specimen of Chinese industry.

It was never printed; even a Chinese emperor, and enthusiastic patron of literature to boot, recoiled before the enormous cost of cutting such a work on blocks. It was however transcribed for printing, and there appear to have been at one time three copies in existence. Two of these perished at Nanking with the downfall of the dynasty in 1644, and the third was in great part destroyed in Peking during the siege of the Legations in 1900. Odd volumes have been preserved, and bear ample witness to the extraordinary character of the achievement.

This emperor was an ardent Buddhist, and the priests of that religion were raised to high positions and exerted considerable influence at court. In times of famine there were loud complaints that some ten thousand priests were living comfortably at Peking, while the people of several provinces were reduced to eating bark and grass.

The porcelain of the Ming dynasty is famous all over the world. Early in the sixteenth century a great impetus was given to the art, owing to the extravagant patronage of the court, which was not allowed to pass without openly expressed remonstrance. The practice of the pictorial art was very widely extended, and the list of Ming painters is endless, containing as it does over twelve hundred names, some few of which stand for a high level of success.

Towards the close of the sixteenth century the Portuguese appeared upon the scene, and settled themselves at Macao, the ownership of which has been a bone of contention between China and Portugal ever since. It is a delightful spot, with an excellent climate, not very far from Canton, and was for some time the residence of the renowned poet Camoens. Not far from Macao lies the island of Sancian, where St. Francois Xavier died. He was the first Roman Catholic missionary of more modern times to China, but he never set foot on the mainland. Native maps mark the existence of "Saint's Grave" upon the island, though he was actually buried at Goa. There had previously been a Roman Catholic bishop in Peking so far back as the thirteenth century, from which date it seems likely that Catholic converts have had a continuous footing in the empire.

In 1583, Matteo Ricci, the most famous of all missionaries who have ever reached China, came upon the scene at Canton, and finally, in 1601, after years of strenuous effort succeeded in installing himself at Peking, with the warm support of the emperor himself, dying there in 1610. Besides reforming the calendar and teaching geography and science in general, he made a fierce attack upon Buddhism, at the same time wisely leaving Confucianism alone. He was the first to become aware of the presence in China of a Jewish colony, which had been founded in 1163. It was from his writings that truer notions of Chinese civilization than had hitherto prevailed, began to spread in the West. "Mat. Riccius the Jesuite," says Burton in his *Anatomy of Melancholy* (1651), "and some others, relate of the industry of the Chinaes most populous countreys, not a beggar, or an idle person to be seen, and how by that means they prosper and flourish."

In 1625 an important find was made. A large tablet, with a long inscription in Chinese and a shorter one in Syraic, was discovered in central China. The inscription, in an excellent state of preservation, showed that the tablet had been set up in A.D. 781 by Nestorian missionaries, and gave a general idea of the object and scope of the Christian religion. The genuineness of this tablet was for many years in dispute—Voltaire, Renan, and others of lesser fame, regarding it as a pious fraud—but has now been established beyond any possibility of doubt; its value indeed is so great that an attempt was made quite recently to carry it off to America. Nestorian Christianity is mentioned by Marco Polo, but disappears altogether after the thirteenth century, without leaving any trace in Chinese literature of its once flourishing condition.

The last emperor of the Ming dynasty meant well, but succumbed to the stress of circumstances. Eunuchs and over-taxation brought about the stereotyped consequence—rebellion; rebellion, too, headed by an able commander, whose successive victories soon enabled him to assume the Imperial title. In the capital all was confusion. The treasury was empty; the garrison were too few to man the walls; and the ministers were anxious to secure each his own safety. On April 9, 1644, Peking fell. During the previous night the emperor, who had refused to flee, slew the eldest princess, commanded the empress to commit suicide, and sent his three sons into hiding. At dawn the bell was struck for the court to assemble; but no one came. His Majesty then ascended the Coal Hill in the palace grounds, and wrote a last decree on the lapel of his robe: "WE, poor in virtue and of contemptible personality, have incurred the wrath of God on high. My ministers have deceived me. I am ashamed to meet my ancestors; and therefore I myself take off my crown, and with my hair covering my face await dismemberment at the hands of the rebels. Do not hurt a single one of my people." He then hanged himself, as also did one faithful eunuch; and his body, together with that of the empress, was reverently encoffined by the rebels.

So ended the Ming dynasty, of glorious memory, but not in favor of the rebel commander, who was driven out of Peking by the Manchus and was ultimately slain by local militia in a distant province.

The subjugation of the empire by the victors, who had the disadvantage of being an alien race, was effected with comparative ease and rapidity. It was carried out by a military occupation of the country, which has survived the original necessity, and is part of the system of government at the present day. Garrisons of Tartar troops were stationed at various important centers of population, each under the command of an officer of the highest military grade, whose duty it was to co-operate with, and at the same time watch and act as a check upon, the high authorities employed in the civil administration. Those Tartar garrisons still occupy the same positions; and the descendants of the first battalions, with occasional reinforcements from Peking, live side by side and in perfect harmony with the strictly Chinese populations, though the two races do not intermarry except in very rare cases. These Bannermen, as they are called, in reference to eight banners or corps under which they are marshaled, may be known by their square heavy faces, which contrast strongly with the sharper and more astute-looking physiognomies of the Chinese. They speak the dialect of Peking, now regarded as the official or "mandarin" language, just as the dialect of Nanking was, so long as that city remained the capital of the empire.

In many respects the conquering Tartars have been themselves conquered by the people over whom they set themselves to rule. They have adopted the language, written and colloquial, of China; and they are fully as proud as the purest-blooded Chinese of the vast literature and glorious traditions of those past dynasties of which they have made themselves joint heirs. Manchu, the language of the conquerors, is still kept alive at Peking. By a fiction, it is supposed to be the language of the sovereign; but the emperors of China have now in their youth to make a study of Manchu, and so do the official interpreters and others whose duty it is to translate from Chinese into Manchu all documents submitted to what is called the "sacred glance" of His Majesty. In a similar sense, until quite a recent date, skill in archery was required of every Bannerman; and it was undoubtedly a great wrench when the once fatally effective weapon was consigned to an unmerited oblivion. But though Bannermen can no longer shoot with the bow and arrow, they still continue to draw monthly allowances from state funds, as an hereditary right obtained by conquest.

Of the nine emperors of the Manchu, or Great Ch'ing dynasty, who have already occupied the dragon throne and have become "guests on high," two are deserving of special mention as fit to be ranked among the wisest and best rulers the world has ever known. The Emperor K'ang

Hsi (*Khahng Shee*) began his reign in 1662 and continued it for sixty-one years, a division of time which has been in vogue for many centuries past. He treated the Jesuit Fathers with kindness and distinction, and availed himself in many ways of their scientific knowledge. He was an extraordinarily generous and successful patron of literature. His name is inseparably connected with the standard dictionary of the Chinese language, which was produced under his immediate supervision. It contains over forty thousand words, not a great number as compared with European languages which have coined innumerable scientific terms, but even so, far more than are necessary either for daily life or for literary purposes. These words are accompanied in each case by appropriate quotations from the works of every age and of every style, arranged chronologically, thus anticipating to some extent the "historical principles" in the still more wonderful English dictionary by Sir James Murray and others, now going through the press. But the greatest of all the literary achievements planned by this emperor was a general encyclopedia, not indeed on quite such a colossal scale as that one produced under the Ming dynasty and already described, though still of respectable dimensions, running as it does in a small-sized edition to 1,628 octavo volumes of about 200 pages to each. The term encyclopedia must not be understood in precisely the same sense as in Western countries. A Chinese encyclopedia deals with a given subject not by providing an up-to-date article written by some living authority, but by exhibiting extracts from authors of all ages, arranged chronologically, in which the subject in question is discussed. The range of topics, however, is such that the above does not always apply—as, for instance, in the biographical section, which consists merely of lives of eminent men taken from various sources. In the great encyclopedia under consideration, in addition to an enormous number of lives of men, covering a period of three thousand years, there are also lives of over twenty-four thousand eminent women, or nearly as many as all the lives in our own *National Dictionary of Biography*. An original copy of this marvelous production,

124

which by the way is fully illustrated, may be seen at the British Museum; a small-sized edition, more suitable for practical purposes and printed from movable type, was issued about twenty years ago.

Skipping an emperor under whose reign was initiated that violent persecution of Roman Catholics which has continued more or less openly down to the present day, we come to the second of the two monarchs before mentioned, whose long and beneficent reigns are among the real glories of the present dynasty.

The Emperor Ch'ien Lung (*Loong*) ascended the throne in 1735, when twenty-five years of age; and though less than two hundred years ago, legend has been busy with his person. According to some native accounts, his hands are said to have reached below his knees; his ears touched his shoulders; and his eyes could see round behind his head. This sort of stuff, is should be understood, is not taken from reliable authorities. It cannot be taken from the dynastic history for the simple reason that the official history of a dynasty is not published until the dynasty has come to an end. There is, indeed, a faithful record kept of all the actions of each reigning emperor in turn; good and evil are set down alike, without fear or favor, for no emperor is ever allowed to get a glimpse of the document by which posterity will judge him. Ch'ien Lung had no cause for anxiety on this score; whatever record might leap to light, he never could be shamed. An able ruler, with an insatiable thirst for knowledge, and an indefatigable administrator, he rivals his grandfather's fame as a sovereign and a patron of letters. His one amiable weakness was a fondness for poetry; unfortunately, for his own. His output was enormous so far as number of pieces go; these were always short, and proportionately trivial. No one ever better illustrated one half of the cynical Chinese saying: "We love our own compositions, but other men's wives." He disliked missionaries, and forbade the propagation of the Christian religion.

After ten years of internal reorganization, his reign became a succession of wars, almost all of which were brought to a successful conclusion. His generals led a large army into Nepaul and conquered the Goorkhas, reaching a point only some sixty miles distant from British territory. Burma was forced to pay tribute; Chinese supremacy was established in Tibet; Kuldja and Kashgaria were added to the empire; and rebellions in Formosa and elsewhere were suppressed. In fifty years the population was nearly doubled, and the empire on the whole enjoyed peace and prosperity. In 1750 a Portuguese embassy reached Peking; and was followed by Lord Macartney's famous mission and a Dutch mission in 1793. Two years after the venerable emperor had completed a reign of sixty years, the full Chinese cycle; whereupon he abdicated in favor of his son, and died in 1799.

CHAPTER XI

CHINESE AND FOREIGNERS

A virtue which the Chinese possess in an eminent degree is the rather rare one of gratitude. A Chinaman never forgets a kind act; and what is still more important, he never loses the sense of obligation to his benefactor. Witness to this striking fact has been borne times without number by European writers, and especially by doctors, who have naturally enjoyed the best opportunities for conferring favors likely to make a deep impression. It is unusual for a native to benefit by a cure at the hands of a foreign doctor, and then to go away and make no effort to express his gratitude, either by a subscription to a hospital, a present of silk or tea, or perhaps an elaborate banner with a golden inscription, in which his benefactor's skill is likened to that of the great Chinese doctors of antiquity. With all this, the patient will still think of the doctor, and even speak of him, not always irreverently, as a foreign devil. A Chinaman once appeared at a British Consulate, with a present of some kind, which he had brought from his home a hundred miles away, in obedience to the command of his dying father, who had formerly been cured of ophthalmia by a foreign doctor, and who had told him, on his deathbed, "never to forget the English." Yet this present was addressed in Chinese: "To His Excellency the Great English Devil, Consul X."

The Chinaman may love you, but you are a devil all the same. It is most natural that he should think so. For generation upon generation China was almost completely isolated from the rest of the world. The people of her vast empire grew up under influences unchanged by contact with other peoples. Their ideals became stereotyped from want of other ideals to compare with, and possibly modify, their own. Dignity of deportment and impassivity of demeanor were especially cultivated by the ruling classes. Then the foreign devil burst upon the scene—a being as antagonistic to themselves in every way as it is possible to conceive. We can easily see, from pictures, not intended to be caricatures, what were the chief features of the foreigner as viewed by the Chinaman. Red hair and blue eyes, almost without exception; short and extremely tight clothes; a quick walk and a mobility of body, involving ungraceful positions either sitting or standing; and with an additional feature which the artist could not portray— an unintelligible language resembling the twittering of birds. Small wonder that little children are terrified at these strange beings, and rush shrieking into their cottages as the foreigner passes by. It is perhaps not quite so easy to understand why the Mongolian pony has such a dread of the foreigner and usually takes time to get accustomed to the presence of a barbarian; some ponies, indeed, will never allow themselves to be mounted unless blindfolded. Then there are the dogs, who rush out and bark, apparently without rhyme or reason, at every passing foreigner. The Chinese have a saying that one dog barks at nothing and the rest bark at him; but that will hardly explain the unfailing attack so familiar to every one who has rambled through country villages. The solution of this puzzle was extracted with difficulty from an amiable Chinaman who explained that what the animals, and indeed his fellow-countrymen as well, could not help noticing, was the frowzy and very objectionable smell of all foreigners, which, strangely enough, is the very accusation which foreigners unanimously bring against the Chinese themselves.

Compare these characteristics with the universal black hair and black eyes of men and women throughout China, exclusive of a rare occasional albino; with the long, flowing, loose robes of officials and of the well-to-do; with their slow and stately walk and their rigid formality of position, either sitting or standing. To the Chinese, their own language seems to be the language of the gods; they know they have possessed it for several thousand years, and they know nothing at all of the barbarian. Where does he come from? Where can he come from except from the small islands which fringe the Middle Kingdom, the world, in fact, bounded by the Four Seas? The books tell us that "Heaven is round, Earth is square;" and it is impossible to believe that those books, upon the wisdom of which the Middle Kingdom was founded, can possibly be wrong. Such was a very natural view for the Chinaman to take when first brought really face to face with the West; and such is the view that in spite of modern educational progress is still very widely held. The people of a country do not unlearn in a day the long lessons of the past. He was quite a friendly mandarin, taking a practical view of national dress, who said in conversation: "I can't think why you foreigners wear your clothes so tight; it must be very difficult to catch the fleas."

As an offset against the virtue of gratitude must be placed the deep-seated spirit of revenge which animates all classes. Though not enumerated among their own list of the Seven passions—joy, anger, sorrow, fear, love, hatred and desire—it is perhaps the most over-mastering passion to which the Chinese mind is subject. It is revenge which prompts the unhappy daughter-in-law to throw herself down a well, consoled by the thought of the trouble, if not ruin, she is bringing on her persecutors. Revenge, too, leads a man to commit suicide on the doorstep of some one who has done him an injury, for he well knows what it means to be entangled in the net which the law throws over any one on whose premises a dead body may thus be found. There was once an absurd case of a Chinese woman, who deliberately walked into a pond until the water reached up to her knees, and remained there, alternately putting her lips below the surface, and threatening in a loud voice to drown herself on the spot, as life had been made unbearable by the presence of foreign barbarians. In this instance, had the suicide been carried out, vengeance would have been wreaked in some way on the foreigner by the injured ghost of the dead woman.

The germ of this spirit of revenge, this desire to get on level terms with an enemy, as when a life is extracted for a life, can be traced, strangely enough, to the practice of filial piety and fraternal love, the very cornerstone of good government and national prosperity. In the Book of Rites, which forms a part of the Confucian Canon, and contains rules not only for the performance of ceremonies but also for the guidance of individual conduct, the following passage occurs: "With the slayer of his father, a man may not live under the same sky; against the slayer of his brother, a man must never have to go home to fetch a weapon; with the slayer of his friend, a man may not live in the same state." Being now duly admitted among the works which constitute the Confucian Canon, the above-mentioned Book of Rites enjoys an authority to which it can hardly lay claim on the ground of antiquity. It is a compilation made during the first century B.C., and is based, no doubt, on older existing documents; but as it never passed under the editorship of either Confucius or Mencius, it would be unfair to jump to the conclusion that either of these two sages is in any way responsible for, or would even acquiesce in, a system of revenge, the only result of which would be an endless chain of bloodshed and murder. The Chinese are certainly as constant in their hates as in their friendships. To use a phrase from their own language, if they love a man, they love him to the life; if they hate a man they hate him to the death. As we have already noted, the Old Philosopher urged men to requite evil with good; but Confucius, who was only a mortal himself, and knew the limitations of mortality, substituted for an ideal doctrine the more practical injunction to requite evil with justice. It is to be feared that the Chinese people fall short in practice even of this lower standard. "Be just to your enemy" is a common enough maxim; but one for which only a moderate application can be claimed.

It has often been urged against the Chinese that they have very little idea of time. A friendly Chinaman will call, and stay on so persistently that he often outstays his welcome. This infliction is recognized and felt by the Chinese themselves, who have certain set forms of words by which they politely escape from a tiresome visitor; among their vast stores of proverbs they have also provided one which is much to the point: "Long visits bring short compliments." Also, in contradiction of the view that time is no value to the Chinaman, there are many familiar maxims which say, "Make every inch of time your own!" "Half-an-hour is worth a thousand ounces of silver," etc. An "inch of time" refers to the sundial, which was known to the Chinese in the earliest ages, and was the only means they had for measuring time until the invention or introduction—it is not certain which—of the more serviceable *clepsydra*, or water-clock, already mentioned.

This consists of several large jars of water, with a tube at the bottom of each, placed one above another on steps, so that the tube of an upper jar overhangs the top of a lower jar. The water from the top jar is made to drip through its tube into the second jar, and so into a vessel at the bottom, which contains either the floating figure of a man, or some other kind of index to mark the rise of the water on a scale divided into periods of two hours each. The day and night were originally divided by the Chinese into twelve such periods; but now-a-days watches and clocks are in universal use, and the European division into twenty-four hours prevails everywhere. Formerly, too, sticks of incense, to burn for a certain number of hours, as well as graduated candles, made with the assistance of the water-clock, were in great demand; these have now quite disappeared as time-recorders.

The Chinese year is a lunar year. When the moon has travelled twelve times round the earth, the year is completed. This makes it about ten days short of our solar year; and to bring things right again, an extra month, that is a thirteenth month, is inserted in every three years. When foreigners first began to employ servants extensively, the latter objected to being paid their wages according to the European system, for they complained that they were thus cheated out of a month's wages in every third year. An elaborate official almanac is published annually in Peking, and circulated all over the empire; and in addition to such information as would naturally be looked for in a work of the kind, the public are informed what days are lucky, and what days are unlucky, the right and the wrong days for doing or abstaining from doing this, that, or the other. The anniversaries of the death-days of the sovereigns of the ruling dynasty are carefully noted; for on such days all the government offices are supposed to be shut. Any foreign official who wishes to see a mandarin for urgent business will find it possible to do so, but the visitor can only be admitted through a side-door; the large entrance-gate cannot possibly be opened under any circumstances whatever.

No notice of the Chinese people, however slight or general in character, could very well attain its object unless accompanied by some more detailed account of their etiquette than is to be gathered from the few references scattered over the preceding pages. Correct behavior, whether at court, in the market-place, or in the seclusion of private life, is regarded as of such extreme importance—and breaches of propriety in this sense are always so severely frowned upon—that it behooves the foreigner who would live comfortably and at peace with his Chinese neighbors, to pick up at least a casual knowledge of an etiquette which in outward form is so different from his own, and yet in spirit is so identically the same. A little judicious attention to these matters will prevent much unnecessary friction, leading often to a row, and sometimes to a catastrophe. Chinese philosophers have fully recognized in their writings that ceremonies and salutations and bowings and scrapings and rules of precedence and rules of the road are not of any real value when considered apart from the conditions with which they are usually associated; at the same time they argue that without such conventional restraints, nothing but confusion would result. Consequently, a regular code of etiquette has been produced; but as this deals largely with court and official ceremonial, and a great part of the remainder has long since been quietly ignored, it is more to the point to turn to the unwritten code which governs the masses in their everyday life.

For the foreigner who would mix easily with the Chinese people, it is above all necessary to understand not only that the street regulations of Europe do not apply in China; but also that he will there find a set of regulations which are tacitly agreed upon by the natives, and which, if examined without prejudice, can only be regarded as based on common sense. An ordinary foot-passenger, meeting perhaps a coolie with two buckets of water suspended one at each end of a bamboo pole, or carrying a bag of rice, weighing one, two, or even three hundredweight, is bound to move out of the burden-carrier's path, leaving to him whatever advantages the road may offer. This same coolie, meeting a sedan chair borne by two or more coolies like himself, must at once make a similar concession, which is in turn repeated by the chair-bearers in favor of any one riding a horse. On similar grounds, an empty sedan-chair must give way to one in which there is a passenger; and though not exactly on such rational grounds, it is understood that horse, chair, coolie and foot-passenger all clear the road for a wedding or other procession, as well as for the retinue of a mandarin. A servant, too, should stand at the side of the road to let his master pass. As an exception to the general rule of common sense which is so very noticeable in all Chinese institutions, if only one takes the trouble to look for it, it seems to be an understood thing that a man may not only stand still wherever he pleases in a Chinese thoroughfare, but may even place his burden or barrow, as the fancy seizes him, sometimes right in the fairway, from which point he will coolly look on at the streams of foot-passengers coming and going, who have to make the best of their way round such obstructions. It is partly perhaps on this account that friends who go for a stroll together never walk abreast but always in single file, shouting out their conversation for all the world to hear; this, too, even in the country, where a more convenient formation would often, but not always, be possible. Shopkeepers may occupy the path with tables exposing their wares, and itinerant stall-keepers do not hesitate to appropriate a "pitch" wherever trade seems likely to be brisk. The famous saying that to have freedom we must have order has not entered deeply into Chinese calculations. Freedom is indeed a marked feature of Chinese social life; some small sacrifices in the cause of order would probably enhance rather than diminish the great privileges now enjoyed.

A few points are of importance in the social etiquette of indoor life, and should not be lightly ignored by the foreigner, who, on the other hand, would be wise not to attempt to substitute altogether Chinese forms and ceremonies for his own. Thus, no Chinaman, and, it may be added, no European who knows how to behave, fails to rise from his chair on the entrance of a visitor; and it is further the duty of a host to see that his visitor is actually seated before he sits down himself. It is extremely impolite to precede a visitor, as in passing through a door; and on parting, it is usual to escort him to the front entrance. He must be placed on the left of the host, this having been the post of honor for several centuries, previous to which it was the seat to the right of the host, as with us, to which the visitor was assigned. At such interviews it would not be correct to allude to wives, who are no more to be mentioned than were the queen of Spain's legs.

One singular custom in connection with visits, official and otherwise, ignorance of which has led on many occasions to an awkward moment, is the service of what is called "guest-tea." At his reception by the host every visitor is at once supplied with a cup of tea. The servant brings two cups, one in each hand, and so manages that the cup in his left hand is set down before the guest, who faces him on his right hand, while that for his master is carried across and set down in an exactly opposite sense. The tea-cups are so handed, as it were with crossed hands, even when the host, as an extra mark of politeness, receives that intended for his visitor, and himself places it on the table, in this case being careful to use *both* hands, it being considered extremely impolite to offer anything with one hand only employed. Now comes the point of the "guest-tea," which, as will be seen, it is quite worth while to remember. Shortly after the beginning of the interview, an unwary foreigner, as indeed has often been the case, perhaps because he is thirsty, or because he may think it polite to take a sip of the fragrant drink which has been so kindly provided for him, will raise the cup to his lips. Almost instantaneously he will hear a loud shout outside, and become aware that the scene is changing rapidly for no very evident reason—only too evident, however, to the surrounding Chinese servants, who know it to be their own custom that so soon as a visitor tastes his "guest-tea," it is a signal that he wishes to leave, and that the interview is at an end. The noise is simply a bawling summons to get ready his sedan-chair, and the scurrying of his coolies to be in their places when wanted. There is another side to this quaint custom, which is often of inestimable advantage to a busy man. A host, who feels that everything necessary has been said, and wishes to free himself from further attendance, may grasp his own cup and invite his guest to drink. The same results follow, and the guest has no alternative but to rise and take his leave. In ancient days visitors left their shoes outside the front door, a custom which is still practiced by the Japanese, the whole of whose civilization—this cannot be too strongly emphasized—was borrowed originally from China.

It is considered polite to remove spectacles during an interview, or even when meeting in the street; though as this rather unreasonable rule has been steadily ignored by foreigners, chiefly, no doubt, from unacquaintance with it, the Chinese themselves make no attempt to observe it so far as foreigners are concerned. In like manner, it is most unbecoming for any "read-book man," no matter how miserably poor he is, to receive a stranger, or be seen himself abroad, in short clothes; but this rule, too, is often relaxed in the presence of foreigners, who wear short clothes themselves. Honest poverty is no crime in China, nor is it in any way regarded as cause for shame; it is even more amply redeemed by scholarship than is the case in Western countries. A man who has gained a degree moves on a different level from the crowd around him, so profound is the respect shown to learning. If a foreigner can speak Chinese intelligibly, his character as a barbarian begins to be perceptibly modified; and if to the knack of speech he adds a tolerable acquaintance with the sacred characters which form the written language, he becomes transfigured, as one in whom the influence of the holy men of old is beginning to prevail over savagery and ignorance.

It is not without reason that the term "sacred" is applied above to the written words or characters. The Chinese, recognizing the extraordinary results which have been brought about, silently and invisibly, by the operation of written symbols, have gradually come to invest these symbols with a spirituality arousing a feeling somewhat akin to worship. A piece of paper on which a single word has once been written or printed, becomes something other than paper with a black mark on it. It may not be lightly tossed about, still less trampled underfoot; it should be reverently destroyed by fire, here again used as a medium of transmission to the great Beyond; and thus its spiritual essence will return to those from whom it originally came. In the streets of a Chinese city, and occasionally along a frequented highroad, may be seen small ornamental structures into which odd bits of paper may be thrown and burnt, thus preventing a desecration so painful to the Chinese mind; and it has often been urged against foreigners that because they are so careless as to what becomes of their written and printed paper, the matter contained in foreign documents and books must obviously be of no great value. It is even considered criminal to use printed matter for stiffening the covers or strengthening the folded leaves of books; still more so, to employ it in the manufacture of soles for boots and shoes, though in such cases as these the weakness of human nature usually carries the day. Still, from the point of view of the Taoist faith, the risk is too serious to be overlooked. In the sixth of the ten Courts of Purgatory, through one or more of which sinners must pass after death in order to expiate their crimes on earth, provision is made for those who "scrape the gilding from the outside of images, take holy names in vain, show no respect for written paper, throw down dirt and rubbish near pagodas and temples, have in their possession blasphemous or obscene books and do not destroy them, obliterate or tear books which teach man to be good," etc., etc.

In this, the sixth Court, presided over, like all the others, by a judge, and furnished with all the necessary means and appliances for carrying out the sentences, there are sixteen different wards where different punishments are applied according to the gravity of the offence. The wicked shade may be sentenced to kneel for long periods on iron shot, or to be placed up to the neck in filth, or pounded till the blood runs out, or to have the mouth forced open with iron pincers and filled with needles, or to be bitten by rats, or nipped by locusts while in a net of thorns, or have the heart scratched, or be chopped in two at the waist, or have the skin of the body torn off and rolled up into spills for lighting pipes, etc. Similar punishments are awarded for other crimes; and these are to be seen depicted on the walls of the municipal temple, to be found in every large city, and appropriately named the Chamber of Horrors. It is doubtful if such ghastly representations of what is to be expected in the next world have really any deterrent effect upon even the most illiterate of the masses; certainly not so long as health is present and things are generally going well. "The devil a monk" will any Chinaman be when the conditions of life are satisfactory to him.

As has already been stated, his temperament is not a religious one; and even the seductions and threats of Buddhism leave him to a great extent unmoved. He is perhaps chiefly influenced by the Buddhist menace of rebirth, possibly as a woman, or worse still as an animal. Belief in such a contingency may act as a mild deterrent under a variety of circumstances; it certainly tends to soften his treatment of domestic animals. Not only because he may some day become one himself, but also because among the mules or donkeys which he has to coerce through long spells of exhausting toil, he may be unwittingly belaboring some friend or acquaintance, or even a member of his own particular family. This belief in rebirth is greatly strengthened by a large number of recorded instances of persons who could recall events which had happened in their own previous state of existence, and whose statements were capable of verification. Occasionally, people would accurately describe places and buildings which they could not have visited, while many would entertain a dim consciousness of scenes, sights and sounds, which seemed to belong to some other than the present life. There is a record of one man who could remember having been a horse, and who vividly recalled the pain he had suffered when riders dug their knees hard into his sides. This, too, in spite of the administration in Purgatory of a cup of forgetfulness, specially designed to prevent in those about to reborn any remembrance of life during a previous birth.

After all, the most awful punishment inflicted in Purgatory upon sinners is one which, being purely mental, may not appeal so powerfully to the masses as the coarse tortures mentioned above. In the fifth Court, the souls of the wicked are taken to a terrace from which they can hear and see what goes on in their old homes after their own deaths. "They see their last wishes disregarded, and their instructions disobeyed. The property they scraped together with so much trouble is dissipated and gone. The husband thinks of taking another wife; the widow meditates second nuptials. Strangers are in possession of the old estate; there is nothing to divide amongst the children. Debts long since paid are brought again for settlement, and the survivors are called upon to acknowledge false claims upon the departed. Debts owed are lost for want of evidence, with endless recriminations, abuse, and general confusion, all of which falls upon the three families—father's, mother's, and wife's—connected with the deceased. These in their anger speak ill of him that is gone. He sees his children become corrupt, and friends fall away. Some, perhaps, may stroke the coffin and let fall a tear, departing quickly with a cold smile. Worse than that, the wife sees her husband tortured in gaol; the husband sees his wife a victim to some horrible disease, lands gone, houses destroyed by flood or fire, and everything in an unutterable plight—the reward of former sins."

Confucius declined absolutely to discuss the supernatural in any form or shape, his one object being to improve human conduct in this life, without attempting to probe that state from which man is divided by death. At the same time, he was no scoffer; for although he declared that "the study of the supernatural is injurious indeed," and somewhat cynically bade his followers "show respect to spiritual beings, but keep them at a distance," yet in another passage we read: "He who offends against God has no one to whom he can pray." Again, when he was seriously ill, a disciple asked if he might offer up prayer. Confucius demurred to this, pointing out that he himself had been praying for a considerable period; meaning thereby that his life had been one long prayer.

CHAPTER XII

THE OUTLOOK

There is a very common statement made by persons who have lived in China—among the people, but not of them—and the more superficial the acquaintance, the more emphatically is the statement made, that the ordinary Chinaman, be he prince or peasant, offers to the Western observer an insoluble puzzle in every department of his life. He is, in fact, a standing enigma; a human being, it may be granted, but one who can no more be classed than his unique monosyllabic language, which still stands isolated and alone.

This estimate is largely based upon some exceedingly false inferences. It seems to be argued that because, in a great many matters, the Chinaman takes a diametrically opposite view to our own, he must necessarily be a very eccentric fellow; but as these are mostly matters of convention, the argument is just as valid against us as against him. "Strange people, those foreigners," he may say, and actually does say; "they make their compass point north instead of south. They take off their hats in company instead of keeping them on. They mount a horse on its left instead of on its right side. They begin dinner with soup instead of dessert, and end it with dessert instead of soup. They drink their wine cold instead of hot. Their books all open at the wrong end, and the lines in a page are horizontal instead of vertical. They put their guests on the right instead of on the left, though it is true that we did that until several hundred years ago. Their music, too, is so funny, it is more like noise; and as for their singing, it is only very loud talking. Then their women are so immodest; striding about in ball-rooms with very little on, and embracing strange men in a whirligig which they call dancing, but very unlike the dignified movements which our male dancers exhibit in the Confucian temple. Their men and women shake hands, though know from our sacred Book of Rites that men and women should not even pass things from one to another, for fear their hands should touch. Then, again, all foreigners, sometimes the women also, carry sticks, which can only be for beating innocent people; and their so-called mandarins and others ride races and row boats, instead of having coolies to do these things for them. They are strange people indeed; very clever at cunning, mechanical devices, such as fire-ships, fire-carriages, and air-cars; but extremely ferocious and almost entirely uncivilized."

Such would be a not exaggerated picture of the mental attitude of the Chinaman towards his enigma, the foreigner. From the Chinaman's imperturbable countenance the foreigner seeks in vain for some indications of a common humanity within; and simply because he has not the wit to see it, argues that it is not there. But there it is all the time. The principles of general morality, and especially of duty towards one's neighbor, the restrictions of law, and even the conventionalities of social life, upon all of which the Chinaman is more or less nourished from his youth upwards, remain, when accidental differences have been brushed away, upon a bed-rock of ground common to both East and West; and it is difficult to see how such teachings could possibly turn out a race of men so utterly in contrast with the foreigner as the Chinese are usually supposed to be. It is certain that anything like a full and sincere observance of the Chinese rules of life would result in a community of human beings far ahead of the "pure men" dreamt of in the philosophy of the Taoists.

As has already been either stated or suggested, the Chinese seem to be actuated by precisely the same motives which actuate other peoples. They delight in the possession of wealth and fame, while fully alive to the transitory nature of both. They long even more for posterity, that the ancestral line may be carried on unbroken. They find their chief pleasures in family life, and in the society of friends, of books, of mountains, of flowers, of pictures, and of objects dear to the collector and the connoisseur. Though a nation of what the Scotch would call "sober eaters," they love the banquet hour, and to a certain extent verify their own saying that "Man's heart is next door to his stomach." In centuries past a drunken nation, some two to three hundred years ago they began to come under the influence of opium, and the abuse of alcohol dropped to a minimum. Opium smoking, less harmful a great deal than opium eating, took the place of drink, and became the national vice; but the extent of its injury to the people has been much exaggerated, and is not to be compared with that of alcohol in the West. It is now, in consequence of recent legislation, likely to disappear, on which result there could be nothing but the warmest congratulations to offer, but for the fact that something else, more insidious and deadly still, is rapidly taking its place. For a time, it was thought that alcohol might recover its sway, and it is still quite probable that human cravings for stimulant of some kind will find a partial relief in that direction. The present enemy, however, and one that demands serious and immediate attention, is morphia, which is being largely imported into China in the shape of a variety of preparations suitable to the public demand. A passage from opium to morphia would be worse, if possible, than from the frying-pan into the fire.

The question has often been asked, but has never found a satisfactory answer, why and how it is that Chinese civilization has persisted through so many centuries, while other civilizations, with equal if not superior claims to permanency, have been broken up and have disappeared from the sites on which they formerly flourished. Egypt may be able to boast of a high level of culture at a remoter date than we can reach through the medium of Chinese records, for all we can honestly claim is that the Chinese were a remarkably civilized nation a thousand years before Christ. That was some time before Greek civilization can be said to have begun; yet the Chinese nation is with us still, and but for contact with the Western barbarian, would be leading very much the same life that it led so many centuries ago.

Some would have us believe that the bond which has held the people together is the written language, which is common to the whole Empire, and which all can read in the same sense, though the pronunciation of words varies in different provinces as much as that of words in English, French, or German. Others have suggested that to the teachings of Confucius, which have outlived the competition of Taoism, Buddhism and other faiths, China is indebted for the tie which has knitted men's hearts together, and enabled them to defy any process of disintegration. There is possibly some truth in all such theories; but these are incomplete unless a considerable share of the credit is allowed to the spirit of personal freedom which seems to breathe through all Chinese institutions, and to unite the people in resistance to every form of oppression. The Chinese have always believed in the divine right of kings; on the other hand, their kings must bear themselves as kings, and live up to their responsibilities as well as to the rights they claim. Otherwise, the obligation is at an end, and their subjects will have none of them. Good government exists in Chinese eyes only when the country is prosperous, free from war, pestilence and famine. Misgovernment is a sure sign that God has withdrawn His mandate from the emperor, who is no longer fit to rule. It then remains to replace the emperor by one who is more worthy of Divine favor, and this usually means the final overthrow of the dynasty.

The Chinese assert their right to put an evil ruler to death, and it is not high treason, or criminal in any way, to proclaim this principle in public. It is plainly stated by the philosopher Mencius, whose writings form a portion of the Confucian Canon, and are taught in the ordinary course to every Chinese youth. One of the feudal rulers was speaking to Mencius about a wicked emperor of eight hundred years back, who had been attacked by a patriot hero, and who had perished in the flames of his palace. "May then a subject," he asked, "put his sovereign to death?" To which Mencius replied that any one who did violence to man's natural charity of heart, or failed altogether in his duty towards his neighbor, was nothing more than an unprincipled ruffian; and he insinuated that it had been such a ruffian, in fact, not an emperor in the true sense of the term, who had perished in the case they were discussing. Another and most important point to be remembered in any attempt to discover the real secret of China's prolonged existence as a nation, also points in the direction of democracy and freedom. The highest positions in the state have always been open, through the medium of competitive examinations, to the humblest peasant in the empire. It is solely a question of natural ability coupled with an intellectual training; and of the latter, it has already been shown that there is no lack at the disposal of even the poorest. China, then, according to a high authority, has always been at the highest rung of the democratic ladder; for it was no less a person than Napoleon who said: "Reasonable democracy will never aspire to anything more than obtaining an equal power of elevation for all."

In order to enforce their rights by the simplest and most bloodless means, the Chinese have steadily cultivated the art of combining together, and have thus armed themselves with an immaterial, invisible weapon which simply paralyses the aggressor, and ultimately leaves them masters of the field. The extraordinary part of a Chinese boycott or strike is the absolute fidelity by which it is observed. If the boatmen or chair-coolies at any place

144

strike, they all strike; there are no blacklegs. If the butchers refuse to sell, they all refuse, entirely confident in each other's loyalty. Foreign merchants who have offended the Chinese guilds by some course of action not approved by those powerful bodies, have often found to their cost that such conduct will not be tolerated for a moment, and that their only course is to withdraw, sometimes at considerable loss, from the untenable position they had taken up. The other side of the medal is equally instructive. Some years ago, the foreign tea-merchants at a large port, in order to curb excessive charges, decided to hoist the Chinese tea-men, or sellers of tea, with their own petard. They organized a strict combination against the tea-men, whose tea no colleague was to buy until, by what seemed to be a natural order of events, the tea-men had been brought to their knees. The tea-men, however, remained firm, their countenances impassive as ever. Before long, the tea-merchants discovered that some of their number had broken faith, and were doing a roaring business for their own account, on the terms originally insisted on by the tea-men.

There is no longer any doubt that China is now in the early stages of serious and important changes. Her old systems of education and examination are to be greatly modified, if not entirely remodeled. The distinctive Chinese dress is to be shorn of two of its most distinguishing features—the *queue* of the man and the small feet of the woman. The coinage is to be brought more into line with commercial requirements. The administration of the law is to be so improved that an honest demand may be made— as Japan made it some years back—for the abolition of extra-territoriality, a treaty obligation under which China gives up all jurisdiction over resident foreigners, and agrees that they shall be subject, civilly and criminally alike, only to their own authorities. The old patriarchal form of government, autocratic in name but democratic in reality, which has stood the Chinese people in such good stead for an unbroken period of nearly twenty-two centuries, is also to change with the changes of the hour, in the hope that a new era will be inaugurated, worthy to rank with the best days of a glorious past.

And here perhaps it may be convenient if a slight outline is given of the course marked out for the future. China is to have a "constitution" after the fashion of most foreign nations; and her people, whose sole weapon of defense and resistance, albeit one of deadly efficiency, has hitherto been combination of the masses against the officials set over them, are soon to enjoy the rights of representative government. By an Imperial decree, issued late in 1907, this principle was established; and by a further decree, issued in 1908, it was ordered that at the end of a year provincial assemblies, to deliberate on matters of local government, were to be convened in all the provinces and certain other portions of the empire, as a first step towards the end in view. Membership of these assemblies was to be gained by election, coupled with a small property qualification; and the number of members in each assembly was to be in proportion to the number of electors in each area, which works out roughly at about one thousand electors to each representative. In the following year a census was to be taken, provincial budgets were to be drawn up, and a new criminal code was to be promulgated, on the strength of which new courts of justice were to be opened by the end of the third year. By 1917, there was to be a National Assembly or Parliament, consisting of an Upper and Lower House, and a prime minister was to be appointed.

On the 14th of October 1909 these provincial assemblies met for the first time. The National Assembly was actually opened on the 3rd of October 1910; and in response to public feeling, an edict was issued a month later ordering the full constitution to be granted within three years from date. It is really a single chamber, which contains the elements of two. It is composed of about one hundred members, appointed by the Throne and drawn from certain privileged classes, including thirty-two high officials and ten distinguished scholars, together with the

146

same number of delegates from the provinces. Those who obtain seats are to serve for three years, and to have their expenses defrayed by the state. It is a consultative and not an executive body; its function is to discuss such subjects as taxation, the issue of an annual budget, the amendment of the law, etc., all of which subjects are to be approved by the emperor before being submitted to this assembly, and also to deal with questions sent up for decision from the provincial assemblies. Similarly, any resolution to be proposed must be backed by at least thirty members, and on being duly passed by a majority, must then be embodied in a memorial to the Throne. For passing and submitting resolutions which may be classed under various headings as objectionable, the assembly can at once be dissolved by Imperial edict.

There are, so far, no distinct parties in the National Assembly, that is, as regards the places occupied in the House. Men of various shades of opinion, Radicals, Liberals and Conservatives, are all mixed up together. The first two benches are set aside for representatives of the nobility, with precedence from the left of the president round to his right. Then come officials, scholars and leading merchants on the next two benches. Behind them, again, on four rows of benches, are the delegates from the provincial assemblies. There is thus a kind of House of Lords in front, with a House of Commons, the representatives of the nation, at the back. The leanings of the former class, as might be supposed, are mostly of a conservative tendency, while the sympathies of the latter are rather with progressive ideas; at the same time, there will be found among the Lords a certain sprinkling of Radicals, and among the Commons not a few whose views are of an antiquated, not to say reactionary, type.

With the above scheme the Chinese people are given to understand quite clearly that while their advice in matters concerning the administration of government will be warmly welcomed, all legislative power will remain, as heretofore, confined to the emperor alone. At the first

147

blush, this seems like giving with one hand and taking away with the other; and so perhaps it would work out in more than one nation of the West. But those who know the Chinese at home know that when they offer political advice they mean it to be taken. The great democracy of China, living in the greatest republic the world has ever seen, would never tolerate any paltering with national liberties in the present or in the future, any more than has been the case in the past. Those who sit in the seats of authority at the capital are far too well acquainted with the temper of their countrymen to believe for a moment that, where such vital interests are concerned, there can be anything contemplated save steady and satisfactory progress towards the goal proposed. If the ruling Manchus seize the opportunity now offered them, then, in spite of simmering sedition here and there over the empire, they may succeed in continuing a line which in its early days had a glorious record of achievement, to the great advantage of the Chinese nation. If, on the other hand, they neglect this chance, there may result one of those frightful upheavals from which the empire has so often suffered. China will pass again through the melting-pot, to emerge once more, as on all previous occasions, purified and strengthened by the process.

BIBLIOGRAPHY

1. *The Chinese Classics*, by James Legge, D.D., late Professor of Chinese at Oxford.

A translation of the whole of the Confucian Canon, comprising the Four Books in which are given the discourses of Confucius and Mencius, the Book of History, the Odes, the Annals of Confucius' native State, the Book of Rites, and the Book of Changes.

2. *The Ancient History of China*, by F. Hirth, Ph.D., Professor of Chinese at Columbia University, New York.

A sketch of Chinese history from fabulous ages down to 221 B.C., containing a good deal of information of an antiquarian character, and altogether placing in its most attractive light what must necessarily be rather a dull period for the general reader.

3. *China*, by E. H. Parker, Professor of Chinese at Victoria University, Manchester.

A general account of China, chiefly valuable for commercial and statistical information, sketch-maps of ancient trade-routes, etc.

4. *A Chinese Biographical Dictionary*, by H. A. Giles, LL.D., Professor of Chinese at the University of Cambridge.

This work contains 2579 short lives of Chinese Emperors, statesmen, generals, scholars, priests, and other classes, including some women, from the earliest times down to the present day, arranged alphabetically.

5. *A Comprehensive Geography of the Chinese Empire*, by L. Richard.

This work is rightly named "comprehensive," for it contains a great deal of information which cannot be strictly classed as geographical, all of which, however, is of considerable value to the student.

6. *Descriptive Sociology (Chinese)*, by E. T. C. Werner, H.B.M. Consul at Foochow.

A volume of the series initiated by Herbert Spenger. It consists of a large number of sociological facts grouped and arranged in chronological order, and is of course purely a work of reference.

7. *A History of Chinese Literature*, by H. A. Giles.

Notes on two or three hundred writers of history, philosophy, biography, travel, poetry, plays, fiction, etc., with a large number of translated extracts grouped under the above headings and arranged in chronological order.

8. *Chinese Poetry in English Verse*, by H. A. Giles.

Rhymed translations of nearly two hundred short poems from the earliest ages down to the present times.

9. *An Introduction to the History of Chinese Pictorial Art*, by H. A. Giles.

Notes on the lives and works of over three hundred painters of all ages, chiefly translated from the writings of Chinese art-critics, with sixteen reproductions of famous Chinese pictures.

10. *Scraps from a Collector's Note-book*, by F. Hirth.

Chiefly devoted to notes on painters of the present dynasty, 1644- 1905, with twenty-one reproductions of famous pictures, forming a complementary supplement to No. 9.

11. *Religions of Ancient China*, by H. A. Giles.

A short account of the early worship of one God, followed by brief notices of Taoism, Buddhism, Nestorian Christianity, Mahommedanism, and other less well-known faiths which have been introduced at various dates into China.

12. *Chinese Characteristics*, by the Rev. Arthur Smith, D.D.

A humorous but at the same time serious examination into the modes of thought and springs of action which peculiarly distinguish the Chinese people.

13. *Village Life in China*, by the Rev. Arthur Smith.

The scope of this work is sufficiently indicated by its title.

14. *China under the Empress Dowager*, by J. O. Bland, and E. Backhouse.

An interesting account of Chinese Court Life between 1860 and 1908, with important sidelights on the Boxer troubles and the Siege of the Legations in 1900.

15. *The Imperial History of China,* by Rev. J. Macgowan.

A short and compact work on a subject which has not been successfully handled.

16. *Indiscreet Letters from Peking,* by B. Putnam Weale.

Though too outspoken to meet with general approbation, this work is considered by many to give the most faithful account of the Siege of the Legations, as seen by an independent witness.

17. *Buddhism as a Religion,* by H. Hackmann, Lic. Theol.

A very useful volume, translated from the German, showing the various developments of Buddhism in different parts of the world.

18. *Chuang Tzu,* by H. A. Giles.

A complete translation of the writings of the leading Taoist philosopher, who flourished in the fourth and third centuries B.C.

www.ingramcontent.com/pod-product-compliance
Lightning Source LLC
Chambersburg PA
CBHW050129280326
41933CB00010B/1301